The
EVERYTHING®
Horseback Riding Book

Dear Reader:

Horses have some sort of hold on the human species. They certainly have a hold on me, considering I have five in my backyard! (Okay, so, my "backyard" is 90 acres.) Many people are simultaneously in awe and petrified of horses. But fear can be eliminated by knowledge. This book will help provide the appropriate knowledge.

Good books on horseback riding abound. Some are even similar to this one. But what makes each book different is the author's unique perspective. I've never been accused of being shy about voicing my opinion of the importance of learning good horsemanship.

When I am trying to work on a problem with a horse, I am more inclined to learn how to refine my horsemanship rather than to turn to a piece of equipment. In my opinion, use of equipment such as a curb bit or tight noseband only masks the symptom, it doesn't address the problem. But in this book, I don't ignore common equipment since you will certainly run across these things; so when something like a "tie down" is discussed in this book you will know where I stand on it!

There's a lot of basic horse stuff you won't find here. I am being arrogant enough to presume you have read my previous book, *The Everything® Horse Book*, which covers information such as breeds and nutrition. This book is about *riding* the horse.

Let's saddle up and have some fun!

The EVERYTHING® Series

Editorial

Publishing Director	Gary M. Krebs
Associate Managing Editor	Laura M. Daly
Associate Copy Chief	Brett Palana-Shanahan
Acquisitions Editor	Kate Burgo
Development Editor	Karen Johnson Jacot
Associate Production Editor	Casey Ebert

Production

Director of Manufacturing	Susan Beale
Associate Director of Production	Michelle Roy Kelly
Cover Design	Paul Beatrice Matt LeBlanc
Design and Layout	Colleen Cunningham Holly Curtis Erin Dawson Sorae Lee
Series Cover Artist	Barry Littmann

THE
EVERYTHING®
HORSEBACK
RIDING BOOK

Step-by-step instruction
for riding like a pro

Cheryl Kimball

Adams Media
Avon, Massachusetts

*To all those riders, novice or experienced, who feel that their
horsemanship could always get better, and, as always, to horses
that do their very best to tolerate the human learning process.*

An Everything® Series Book.
Everything® and everything.com® are registered trademarks of F+W Publications, Inc.

Published by Adams Media, an F+W Publications Company
57 Littlefield Street, Avon, MA 02322 U.S.A.
www.adamsmedia.com

ISBN: 1-59337-426-7

Printed in the United States of America.

J I H G F E D C B A

Library of Congress Cataloging-in-Publication Data
Kimball, Cheryl.
The everything horseback riding book / Cheryl Kimball.
p.   cm.
(An everything series book)
ISBN 1-59337-426-7
1. Horsemanship. I. Title. II. Series: Everything series.
SF309.K44 2005
798.2—dc22
2005015479

This publication is designed to provide accurate and authoritative information with regard to the subject matter covered. It is sold with the understanding that the publisher is not engaged in rendering legal, accounting, or other professional advice. If legal advice or other expert assistance is required, the services of a competent professional person should be sought.

—From a *Declaration of Principles* jointly adopted by a Committee of the American Bar Association and a Committee of Publishers and Associations

Many of the designations used by manufacturers and sellers to distinguish their products are claimed as trademarks. Where those designations appear in this book and Adams Media was aware of a trademark claim, the designations have been printed with initial capital letters.

*This book is available at quantity discounts for bulk purchases.
For information, please call 1-800-872-5627.*

Contents

The Natural Aids / 139

Artificial Aids / 151

Balance, Timing, Feel, and Awareness / 163

Arena Work / 175

Trail Riding / 187

Competition / 203

Acknowledgments

I would first like to thank the many horses who have tolerated me over the years as I learned to become a better rider. I have a long way to go but I couldn't have come this far without the patience (and in some cases the lack of it!) of each and every one.

Equally as patient in my progress as a rider have been the clinicians I have ridden with. They have pushed me when I needed it, supported me when I needed that, and allowed me to drift and learn on my own when that seemed the best way. The best way I know to thank them is to continue to ride with them and to simply ride.

As always, my group of "horse friends" is invaluable to me in all my equine endeavors. We bounce ideas off each other and encourage and support each other with advice, empathy, and encouragement.

Thanks to Gena McGrath, Gelinas Farm, and the folks at David & Charles who all have helped in what ended up being a difficult search for the right photos at the right resolution showing the right thing. Kate Burgo at Adams Media has been a most patient editor. And all the people behind the scenes who I don't get to interact with also have my appreciation.

Top Ten Reasons
to Ride Horses

1. You've wanted to ride ever since you were little.

2. It's a perfect excuse to spend time in a barn.

3. Learn something new and be challenged every time you ride.

4. Be outside a lot.

5. Great excuse to buy some cool clothes.

6. You can eat more since you expend a lot of calories.

7. Impress your nonriding friends.

8. Keep physically fit without going to the gym.

9. Meet great people.

10. Have a meaningful relationship with a half-ton animal.

Introduction

▶ YOU ARE READING THIS BOOK so the idea of riding horses has piqued your interest. If you fit into the usual profile, this interest in riding has been percolating for a while—whether you are fourteen years old or forty-five! It's not hard to understand.

Horses are a lot of things. They are huge, which makes them fascinating. They are simple yet can seem very complicated. And they are beautiful. Sleek coats, flowing manes, soft muzzles—who wouldn't want to be around them?

Horses are also inherently dangerous to humans. If you want to spend time around horses it's your responsibility to learn how to interact with a horse in the safest way possible. That doesn't mean simply being sure to always wear a helmet when you ride, although that is certainly a smart thing to do. Being safe around horses entails learning what is important to a horse and respecting that—and expecting respect from the horse in return.

There's no need for being stepped on all the time or being kicked or bitten. A horse will do all these things if he doesn't understand the parameters of your relationship. There's also no need to force the horse to comply with your wishes by using harsh equipment, training, and riding techniques. Improve your horsemanship and you will get what you want from your horse.

It's very important for a horse is to get along with its rider. If you can learn to communicate effectively with a horse, the horse will readily meet you halfway. When you get to that point of mutual respect, you'll have one of the most rewarding relationships in the world.

This book will help you with all of that. Although learning good horsemanship is a lifelong pursuit that isn't possible to treat between the covers of any book no matter how long, the following pages touch upon the important points you will want to consider as you explore the fascinating world of horseback riding.

For some people, horseback riding comes naturally. These people climb into the saddle, the horse starts to move, and the two look like they belong together. Perhaps that describes you. More likely it doesn't.

Most new riders need to learn some techniques and get some experience riding. The value of "saddle time" can't be overestimated. If you are totally brand new to riding and feel like a chimp clinging to the saddle, have faith—one year from now you will look back and be amazed at how far you have come.

And although it can be a little cliché, it's absolutely true when it comes to horseback riding: The journey is more important than the end result. Even the most accomplished horseback riders will tell you that learning good horsemanship is a process that never ends.

Chapter 1

Why Horseback Riding?

There are two kinds of people: those who ride horses, and those who have always wanted to ride horses. Many people are fascinated by horses and their beauty. Learning to ride can be a very fulfilling experience and tons of fun to boot. You don't have to spend lots of money to ride horses—you just have to enjoy the animals and be willing to try it out. Let's get started with what you need to know about horses.

In the Beginning

Although current attitudes toward horses make it difficult to imagine, horses once meant dinner to humans. Early humans were known to run horses over cliffs to their death below, where they would become dinner for several nights. But that began to change as humans started to see horses having value as pack animals and transportation rather than a food source. Once horses became more of an integral part of human life, they found their way to the dinner table less and less often.

Evidence exists that horses were first ridden as much as 5,000 or more years ago. This evidence is in the form of bits found in archaeological dig sites or horse skeletons found that indicate the horse had tooth wear in keeping with bit use.

FACT

The dog-sized horse from which the contemporary horse evolved beginning 55 million years ago was known as *eohippus*, or more formally Hyracotherium.

One curious fact of horse history is that although horses originated on the North American continent they completely disappeared for several thousand years right after the Ice Age around 8,000 years ago. The exact reason for this remains a mystery—perhaps the last horse ran north across the land bridge that connected the North American and Asian continents before the bridge gave way to the ocean. Perhaps a devastating disease decimated the North American continent's horse population. Whatever the cause, the horse returned to North America in great numbers, brought back to the continent by the Spanish Conquistadors in the 1400s. The wild band of horses on the eastern shore of Maryland—the famous Chincoteague ponies—were thought perhaps to be survivors of early Spanish shipwrecks along the east coast.

Today, horses are found all over North America, numbering in the millions in the United States alone.

Horses as a Hobby

Equestrian pursuits are very different from other sports you can become involved in. The main difference is, of course, the horse. Equestrian events are the only recognized sports that involve a live animal.

FACT

Equestrian events are one of the few Olympic events where men and women compete on equal ground. Equestrian sports at the Olympics include three-phase eventing (dressage, stadium jumping, and cross country) and may soon include a Western-style event called "reining." In the ancient Olympic games, there were chariot races including two- and four-horse chariots as well as races in which foals pulled the chariots and another in which mules pulled chariots. Of course, chariot racing is not an event in modern-day Olympic games.

If you're interested in horses but aren't sure where to even begin, you're in the right place. Begin by reading books like this one and magazines about horses, especially magazines that are relevant to your local geographic area. You probably won't find the local equine publications at national chain bookstores, so you might need to go to either a tack shop or a feed store in your area to pick up horse-related local and regional publications. Then start visiting some horse places—lesson barns, boarding facilities, and trail riding establishments are possibilities.

Absorb yourself in as much horse-related stuff as you can fit in. Start to talk with people about the realities of owning and riding horses in your area. At some point, you will either burst if you don't get more involved, or you will find that horseback riding just doesn't interest you as much as you thought it did.

Not everyone who is eager to ride horses needs to own one. There are many angles to approach horseback riding without being completely responsible for one. However, if you are considering purchasing a horse, this is a perfect time to really take stock of your lifestyle, your plans for the future, and the kind of person you are day-to-day. Because, as you'll see further on, horse ownership might be better left to other people.

ALERT!

Beware of getting interested in horses just because one of your friends is. Riding horses is a serious undertaking that you should be doing because you really want to. Although, for the most part, horseback riding is fun, it can be dangerous and exhausting physical work so you really need to be doing it for yourself not for others.

People who don't know much about horses often have the impression that being involved in horseback riding is expensive. It could be, but being involved with horses doesn't have to be overly expensive. The main thing is not to try to keep up with the Joneses; just buy the best you can—whether it's hay, equipment, or lessons—for the money you can budget for your horse hobby. Keep things simple. And make keeping your horse healthy—physically and mentally—a priority. The healthier your horse, the fewer unplanned veterinary bills, which could really add up.

The quickest way to a healthy horse is by feeding the proper amount of grain for his age and activity level, dust-free nutritious hay preferably free-choice, and ample amounts of clean water. Tend to the horse's physical needs by giving him free-choice turnout with a run-in shed, even if the area is a small paddock. This kind of arrangement also helps take care of his mental needs by helping prevent box-stall-created unhealthy habits like weaving and pacing and just plain cooped-up grouchiness.

FACT

Horses have a very small stomach in proportion to their large size. Because of this, they need to have small amounts of food regularly passing through their digestive systems. If the horse eats grain to get a portion of the nutrients he needs, the grain needs to be distributed in small amounts at least twice a day, maybe three times. This is an important thing for the would-be horse owner to consider.

What It Takes to Own a Horse

If you don't like routine, horse ownership is probably not for you. From a health standpoint, horses thrive on routine. Spreading out a twice-daily grain feeding as close to twelve hours apart as possible is important. It's also important to provide hay either free choice or spread out over several feedings throughout the day.

Many people own horses and work a nine-to-five job. They feed before they go to work in the morning and feed when they get home (often with their office clothes still on!), and their horses get along just fine. But it's still a routine. If you work and have horses, it helps to find a neighbor who can come and feed some hay at lunch time, check on the horse, and make sure water buckets are full.

Water is the other key to the horse's diet—it's even more important than hay and grain. Water needs to be clean and free flowing even in winter. To avoid impaction colic—basically, a severe and potentially deadly case of constipation—horses need to keep their food moving through their bodies, and water is what helps keep it moving freely.

If you are willing to be as diligent about feeding and watering your horse (and mucking stalls, having regular horseshoeing/trimming appointments, grooming, annual vaccines, dental work, and occasional emergency veterinary care), as much if not more than you are about riding, then you will do fine caring for a horse.

For those riders who don't live in a rural environment or who don't think the day-to-day care of a horse works within their lifestyle, a boarding establishment is a perfect solution. Depending on where you live, the boarding fees can be quite reasonable, or they can be like having a second mortgage to pay each month.

The good news is that most boarding fees are pretty stable (pardon the pun!). They might go up a bit each year (the cost of maintaining a property used by many people and horses as well as the taxes on such a tract of land is no small figure). However, there are seldom few "add-ons" to add significant amounts to your monthly bill. If you are in a cold climate, there might be a slight fee during winter months to take blankets on and off. Most boarding establishments require that you allow them to put your horse on their deworming schedule so they can have the whole barn on the same cycle. And if you can't be there for the vet or the horseshoer, there will be a handling fee for a barn employee to do it for you. Convenience costs money!

E ALERT!

Hay for horses can get expensive. It takes a lot of hay to feed one horse. The rule of thumb is around 150 bales of hay per year per horse. The cost of hay fluctuates wildly from region to region and from season to season. For instance, if you live in northern New England, have adequate storage space, and buy your annual supply of hay from the "first cutting" out of the field in season, you might spend only $300 for your horse's whole year of hay. If you don't have storage, buy "second cut," and have it delivered monthly, you could spend over $800 for one horse's annual hay supply.

In Chapter 6, you will learn a lot about the different ways you can get into riding horses without owning a horse. Leasing, half leasing, borrowing, or simply taking lessons are all fulfilling ways to interact with horses. Again, you must be willing to look very carefully and honestly at your lifestyle and your own personality to decide which way is best for you.

There is no such thing as doing too much research if you are seriously considering buying a horse. Add up all your "one time" needs like manure fork, fencing, and water and feed tubs. Then add in ongoing costs like feed, veterinary, and foot care. Don't forget saddles, bridles, and other riding equipment. Be realistic, but don't go overboard either. You don't need to rush out to buy a truck and trailer—a lot of those kinds of needs depend on where you keep your horse and what you plan to do with him, all of which will develop over time.

The upside to horse ownership, whether you board or keep your horse at home, is that riding is fun. To learn how to get along safely with a half-ton animal is just plain rewarding. The view from the back of a horse is like nothing you've ever witnessed before. Jumping even the smallest jump is exhilarating. And most horse people are as nice as people can be.

Begin to gather a group of trusted friends who are knowledgeable about horses and horseback riding as soon as you start thinking about riding. Your horse's health care team, including a veterinarian, horseshoer, dentist, trainer, and (at the top of the list) you, is an essential part of your equine circle. However, it will be other horse owners like yourself who will provide you with immense amounts of information, advice, and moral support throughout your horse-owning years.

FACT

There are many ways to use your talents and interests while still being involved with horses. Homeopathic medicine has come to the equine world with a vengeance. You can learn about herbal treatments. The energy therapies like massage, reiki, acupressure, and acupuncture are all common therapies used with horses. Learning to build things comes in handy—jumps, fences, stalls. Sewing your own show clothes or knitting warm winter wear is a moneysaving pursuit. Any activity you could imagine could help you to be involved with horses.

Watching Horses

Once you become involved with horses, you will begin to crave horse connections in the other parts of your life. Although it's always good not to become so single-minded that you get boring, you will most likely start to become less interested in attending events and other activities that have nothing to do with horses. There are a lot of horse events and facilities that you can go to to fulfill a need to watch horses, especially if you don't have your own. Here are a few.

The Kentucky Horse Park

Located in the heart of horse racing country in Lexington, Kentucky, the Kentucky Horse Park is a horse lovers' dream come true. Thirty miles of classic white board fencing lace through this working horse farm. The Park has two museums, including the International Museum of the Horse, and as many as fifty different breeds of horses living at the Park. The horse that played Seabiscuit in the movie has retired to the Park. Ongoing demonstrations, trail rides around the park, and daily "horse breed parades" make this a destination point for all those who admire horses. Check out their Web site at *www.imh.com* or call (859) 259-4219 for events.

The Lippizaner Stallions

One place to see magnificent Lippizan horses is at Tempel Farms in Wadsworth, Illinois. Following the intense dressage training of the famed Vienna Spanish Riding School, the farm does a daily hour-long performance. You could tour the farms and have lunch in their tented café. If you are there at the right time of year, you could see the young foals, who start their lives pitch black and then gray before turning to the classic Lippizan white. If you can't make it to Illinois, check the Royal Lippizaner Stallions traveling show schedule at *www.lippizaner.com* or call (407) 366-0366.

The National Cowboy and Western Heritage Museum

This museum celebrating the cultural heritage of the west opened in 1965. It's located in Oklahoma City, Oklahoma, and is a sprawling 200,000 square feet with several galleries and natural features. A fascinating feature of the museum is a walk through a replica of a turn-of-the-twentieth-century Western town, Prosperity Junction, with nineteen buildings. Some of these buildings are two-stories high, and some can be entered by museum visitors. The town has a perpetual timeframe of just after sunset. Plan your visit at *www.nationalcowboymuseum.org* or call (405) 478-2250.

Equine Affaires

Four times a year in four different parts of the country, all-things-horse gather for what has become a premiere horse event called Equine Affaire. Hundreds of tack shops, jewelers, booksellers, and other purveyors of horse-related gear fill the convention halls. Ongoing demonstrations by internationally known clinicians and riders are found in small demonstration arenas throughout the show. Typically four days long, there is so much to see that an overnight stay is recommended. If you stay overnight, be sure to attend the evening performance—usually a fantastic display of horsemanship and fun. For those who have horses to buy for, great sales offer things you need or want from dewormers to horse trailers. The Equine Affaire schedule is mid-November in Massachusetts, early February in California, mid-April in Ohio, and mid-September in Kentucky. Check out ✍*www.equineaffaire.com* for details and to get on their mailing list.

The recreational horse world is predominantly populated by women. Many women would like their husbands, boyfriends, and partners to ride with them, at least once in a while. But since these partners are not as committed to riding as they are, the best thing to put the partner on is a safe, reliable, well educated, and probably older horse. You might even see a horse for sale that is referred to as a good "husband horse."

Livestock Shows

Each year, several national livestock shows take place (and have since the West was won). Many of these events have branched out from their literal beginnings of selling livestock to include English riding events as well as stock dog shows and horse sales. The Grand National Horse, Rodeo, and Livestock Show graces San Francisco's Cow Palace in early November. The National Western Stock Show is held in Denver in mid-January. Also in mid-January is the Fort Worth Stock Show. There are several others, and they can be loads of fun.

Famous Clydesdales

The Budweiser Clydesdales reside in St. Louis, Missouri, at Grant's Farm (✍www.grantsfarm.com). Around thirty-five of the big draft horses are there. The characteristics of the Clydesdales that are chosen to represent Budweiser are strictly regulated. These giant horses stand a minimum of 18 hands (6 feet!). The Farm also has a deer park, concessions, and admission is free.

Chapter 2

What to Wear

Equestrian clothing can be as stylish as you want it to be. Some people wear this kind of clothing just for the fashion statement it makes. But style isn't the only consideration—the right clothing will help you have a more enjoyable (and safer) experience while riding horses. This chapter covers what you need to know about wearing the right clothes to ride.

Buy Good Equipment

You could wear equestrian clothing just to make a fashion statement—some of it's that stylish! Look through most clothing catalogs and you will find boots and jackets called "riding style" that are made to look as if you are headed out with the hounds. Horses, hounds, bugles, foxes, and snaffle bits (although most people don't have a clue what they are!) often adorn scarves and handbags.

However, when you get into riding in any serious way, you will want to wear equestrian clothing because it's made to help you be comfortable while astride a horse. Riding clothing tends to be highly tailored at the waist, hips, and shoulders. This clothing is designed to allow movement where movement happens and to prevent bulk where chafing might occur. And much riding apparel is also designed for safety, some apparel more blatantly so (helmets that protect your head) than others. For instance, leather "roper-style" cowboy boots are made to slip off if you fall off and get a foot caught in a stirrup, opposed to lace-up boots that are tied on tight.

FACT

Retails shops devoted to horseback riders—known as "tack shops"—usually bend over backward to make their customers happy. They know that horseback riders are a devoted crowd who will come back many times a year and spend goodly sums of money. Although you don't want to be considered the resident pest, you shouldn't be shy about making sure you are happy with your purchases. They want your repeat business!

Like with all equipment specific to an activity, buy the best you can afford. That doesn't mean if you are just going to a dude ranch for a week, you should take out a bank loan to outfit yourself. If you are a casual rider taking lessons once a week, you won't need to have top-quality equipment. But higher quality often means better fit, which means you will be more comfortable. And it also often means that equipment designed for safety will have more safety features than inexpensive models.

Ultimately, however, the big thing to keep in mind is that horseback riding is a very physical activity. Observers might think that it's the horse doing all the work, but you won't be fooled for long—your thighs will tell you, your knees will tell you, your hips, arms, and rear end will tell you that the rider has to maintain her side of the activity scale as well as the horse. Good riding gear that is up to the task can have a huge impact on how comfortable all those body parts feel after a couple of hours in the saddle.

Helmets

Helmets are the most important piece of physical safety equipment you will buy. Buy one even if you are just taking lessons. Most of the helmets on the market are ASTM-certified but always check to be 100 percent sure.

Always buy a helmet that is designed for horseback riding—don't use a bicycling helmet, a motorcycling helmet, or a skiing helmet. Helmets are designed specifically from extensive testing that indicates where a horseback rider might be likely to hit in a fall, and where the strongest impact might be—and it's different from sport to sport. Many new horseback riding helmet designs are covering more of back of the head than in the past.

The two most important things after the ASTM certification are fit and comfort. A helmet must fit you right to offer adequate protection. The helmet itself should sit down on your head, not perch on top of it. Most helmets come with pieces of foam padding that stick in to help make them fit better. The strap should be snug around your chin but not choking you, and you should *always* have the strap buckled whenever you are mounted.

Comfort is important because if the helmet isn't comfortable, you won't be as inclined to wear it. If you buy a helmet, ride in it a couple of times, and if you don't like it, bring it back to the tack shop where you bought it. As long as it appears new, and you retained the box and all the packaging and foam parts (and sometimes even if you didn't), the tack shop will be happy to exchange it for another helmet.

You can even accessorize your helmet with helmet covers in bright colors, jockey silk color schemes, or tiger prints—or other things beyond your imagination! Most helmets do come with several ventilation holes to help with comfort.

A helmet is an integral part of an English rider's "uniform." Western riders have never embraced helmets. Cowboys claim the bucket of the cowboy hat offers protection. Those who believe that might have hit their heads one too many times. Wear a helmet no matter what saddle you ride in.

Boots

Riding footwear has come a long way in the past decade or two. The choices no longer are limited to leather cowboy boots for Western riding and tall leather boots for English riding. Apparel companies have come out with sneaker-like riding boots and paddock boots; a clog company is even making a riding shoe. Many riding shoes and boots are so comfortable and so stylish you might begin to find yourself buying all your footwear at the tack shop! Although not the cheapest place to buy shoes, horse riding apparel is made to last and might ultimately be a great value for the price.

You can buy your riding shoes from catalogs as well as from local tack shops, and often you can find great prices in catalogs. But unlike lots of horse care supplies, it can be difficult to get the right fit if you buy shoes and boots through the mail. Sometimes it just pays to drive to the largest tack shop near you and try things on. If the price from a catalog is exceptionally less, then you might want to find your size and then go home and order from the catalog. But don't forget that shipping adds to the cost, and besides, it's always good to support your local tack shop or it might not be there when you really need it.

ALERT!

Put simply, sneakers have no place in a barn. They offer no protection from falling objects or from getting your foot hurt if a horse steps on you. Sneakers have no heel for safe riding, and because they offer no support, they will prove uncomfortable on a long ride. Sneakers are not made to rub against the inside of stirrups for hours on end. They hold odors, and the fabric will deteriorate fast from the strength of manure and urine. Save your sneakers for the tennis court.

Heel!

All footwear intended for horseback riding has a heel. The heel is one of the safety features of an appropriate riding boot. The heel helps your foot from being accidentally poked all the way through the stirrup, which, you will learn in a later chapter, is a very dangerous position for your foot. English and Western riding boots have heels. The newer styles of riding boots, including the sneaker style, have heels. The heel is the deal.

FACT

The word "chaps" is technically pronounced as if it were spelled with an "sh." The word is a shortened derivative of the western shrubby plant "chaparral," which chaps were invented to protect riders from.

Protection

Leather riding boots do provide a modest amount of protection around the barn. Although saddle horses should be respectful enough of humans to keep to their own space and not risk stepping on your feet, it happens. And you will be happy to have at least a leather boot on. And barns themselves are places where sturdy boots can mean the difference between yelling "Ouch!" or being driven off to the emergency room for a puncture wound from a pitch fork.

Style

Cowboys wear cowboy boots. And if you ride Western, you will probably want cowboy boots too. They are comfortable. They are designed to hold spurs if you need to wear spurs. The "roper" style cowboy boot is designed to come off quickly, if necessary. They are leather and hold up well to the wear imposed by horseback riding. If you take good care of them—clean and condition them regularly—they should last you a long while.

Smartly appointed English riders wear tall leather boots. Apparel companies have come out with styles of tall boots that are more casual than the spit-shined black leather riding boots that seem to take twenty minutes each to pull on. Some styles have elasticized gussets that make the calf area more flexible, and they have zippers up the back to make getting them on and off much easier.

You can also choose to wear ankle-high boots (with heels, of course!) that are known as "paddock boots." Paddock boots can be dressed up to look, from a distance, like tall English riding boots by using a pair of "half chaps." Half chaps cover the entire calf area, usually wrapping around and fastening in the back with Velcro®. An elastic band similar to that found on stretch pants loops underneath your boot.

Lastly, there are riding shoes that resemble sneakers, but a look below the surface reveals a shoe much more appropriate than plain tennis shoes. First, and most noticeable, is the critical horseback riding footwear item, the heel. Not visible is a steel shaft in the sole of the shoe. These shoes, however, typically do not offer much protection on the top of the shoe, and the rubber soles have been considered somewhat more slippery on stirrups than leather soles if your feet get wet. But they are very comfortable and seem to be used equally by Western and English riders.

Barn Boots

The boots you wear to do barn chores can be quite different from those you wear to ride—in fact, they *should* be different. If you muck out stalls, either at your own barn or as part of an exchange agreement with a boarding barn, you will want a sturdy pair of rubber-soled boots. There are many different kinds of these boots, and you will want to try a bunch on and find the ones you like the best. However, get recommendations from other barn-chore friends since horse manure and urine will quickly rot the rubber. Sometimes it can be best to buy a cheap pair and replace them every three months since even the best rubber won't last a super long time. Also, as mentioned above, rubber holds the smell of manure and urine so don't plan to store your rubber muck boots in the car! Leave them at the board barn if you can.

Pants

The third critical item in your horseback riding wardrobe is pants. Jeans are *de rigeur* for Western style. Look for jeans with the double seam on the outside of the leg not the inside (for comfort reasons). And buy your riding jeans 4 to 6 inches longer than you wear for street clothes. When you sit in the saddle, you take up a lot of length so if your jeans are the length you normally wear them, your ankles will stick out when you ride.

English riders wear breeches (pronounced "britches"), which are basically stretch pants with reinforced areas in the inner legs and sometimes also the seat to help with wear and with "stickiness" in the saddle. Endurance riders, who often use a saddle that looks like a Western/English hybrid, wear breeches for their long distance riding—they are just plain comfortable!

When buying jeans to ride in, look for those that are made with the flat double seam on the outside of the leg, not on the inseam side. That double layer of denim can chafe uncomfortably anywhere your leg hits the saddle. Wrangler's and women's stretch jeans are two common favorites for Western riders.

Other Clothes

Boots, helmets, and pants are the three most critical items you need to consider when collecting together your riding wardrobe. But there are plenty of other riding items you can shop for 'til you drop! Although sometimes riding accessories might seem to be extraneous, they are mostly tailor-made for equestrian pursuits; you will find that they are cut to be comfortable while sitting in the saddle.

Vests

Vests can be perfect for horseback riding—they are less bulky than a full coat and they keep you warm but not too warm when you are physically active. Riding apparel manufacturers have long recognized the attraction of vests to the riding crowd, and there are many you can choose from, all stylish, all in interesting colors, and all with added features like lots of pockets, reversible sides, and longer back flaps that help keep your hips a little warmer.

If you are getting into jumping in any serious way—perhaps at all—you might want to consider acquiring a safety vest. Like a helmet, safety vests are designed to protect you in a fall. While it's possible to fall off from even the oldest horse that doesn't do much more than walk (that horse could get stung by a bee and sent rocketing, you just never know!), the chances of falling when you get into jumping are simply statistically higher. A vest and a helmet won't guarantee you won't get hurt (Christopher Reeve was wearing a helmet when he fell during a jump, but he still sustained paralyzing injuries), but decreasing the odds can't be a bad idea.

Safety vests cost at least a couple hundred dollars, but calculate this: say, for example, in a lesson you are jumping an average of twenty-five times. And you take two lessons a week. That's fifty jumps. And then you practice on your own a couple of times a week, perhaps jumping another twenty-five times in each practice session. Inside of one week, you could have jumped with a horse 100 times. In two weeks, your $200 safety vest would have cost you $1 per jump! That's not much. If you really don't want to spend a lot, check with a tack shop that specializes in selling used equipment to see if you can get a used vest.

Shirts

Shirts are not nearly as critical an item to consider for riding. Long sleeves are nice even in warm weather since horseback riding often means you are outside a lot, and long sleeves can help protect you from the sun—and from bugs during fly season. The critical factor for comfort when it comes to shirts is for them to be long enough to tuck in well. (If it's not supposed to be tucked in, then it doesn't matter. But if it is, a shirt that is too short is very annoying!)

Undergarments

Again, a seemingly small thing to consider, but bad socks that creep down into your boots can make your feet sore. Riders can look for specially made underwear for the equestrian in catalogs—this underwear is made to prevent discomfort in the sensitive areas that have contact with the saddle. And women might want to consider a sports-type bra, available in any sporting goods store or in many equestrian wear catalogs.

FACT

The most famous cowboy hat is, perhaps, the Stetson, which was first manufactured in 1865. The cowboy's hat has a very practical design. The large brim keeps rain and sun off the face, and the deep bucket can be used to offer your horse a drink or rinse off your face. By the way, the popular name "ten-gallon" hat was a misnomer, the hat bucket holds less than a half gallon!

Accessories

Besides your basic riding wear, there are many accessories you might want to consider to help keep you comfortable while riding.

Scarves

Watch any old Western movie, and you will notice that all the cowboys are wearing scarves. For the working cowboy, a scarf—often known as a "wild rag"—is not a fashion statement, it's an important piece of gear on the open range. The scarf serves the fundamental purpose of helping keep you warm. It also doubles as a shield for the mouth and nose in dry, dusty, and windy conditions. And the other duties a scarf can perform include protection from the sun; a cooling mechanism when soaked in water either just to wash your face or to wrap wet around your neck; and as an emergency bandage for either you or your horse.

Gloves

Horse-related activities are hard on the hands. Leather gets sweaty and dirty; hay is prickly, and hay baling twine digs into the hands. Grooming a horse takes all the dirt off the horse and deposits it on the groomer. Maintaining fences is an integral part of horse care. Barns are full of possible places to cut yourself. The list of possible injuries to your hands is endless. The message is simple: wear gloves.

And wear good sturdy gloves. Figure out what size you take, then order them from horse and farm gear catalogs (see Appendix A for a list of catalogers). Although gloves found in outdoor sports catalogs are often warm and high quality, there aren't many activities that generate the wear and tear of horse work.

For riding, you will find an array of gloves in tack catalogs. Some are made especially for warm weather wear; they might be synthetic or leather with synthetic mesh areas between the fingers or on the back of the hand to give some extra ventilation. For just hacking around on the trails, buy the gloves that you find are the most comfortable.

Again, buying gloves that are made for other sports could work against you. For instance, although you will find gloves with mesh backs and velcro wrist closures in tack shops, don't think that means that you might as well just grab your bicycle touring gloves and use those. You can if you want to, of course, no one will get hurt. But bicycling gloves often have gel pads in the palms which help with comfort if you are leaning on handlebars for 50 miles in a day. But those gel pads will only work against you when it comes to feeling your horse through the reins.

Chaps

Chaps are smooth leather or suede coverings that go over your jeans. They protect your jeans from wear and tear, they help you avoid chafing, and they add a certain amount of "stickiness" to your seat. Like most anything horse-gear related, you can buy them off the rack or get them custom made. And also like anything horse-gear related, when you are first learning how to ride, you can probably get along with a cheaper pair; but once you get a little more experienced, you start to understand the value of higher quality things like custom-made chaps. Your chaps should be short enough that a pair of spurs would clear the cuff but not so short that people ask you if you are waiting for the tide to come in! The leather your chaps are made of must be able to withstand a lot of wear and tear. But the most critical thing in chaps is quality zippers—chaps zip up on the side toward the back. The zippers can be a bit awkward to get to, so if it's hard to zip up under the best of circumstances, it will be even harder with poor quality zippers.

Rain Gear

Most recreational horseback riders don't ride in torrential rain. But if you choose to get into showing, you will find that shows do not get canceled because of rain. Or maybe you signed up for a trail ride that required six hours driving to a different state and a couple of nights in a hotel. If you wake up the morning of the ride and it's raining, you probably will feel inclined to still go.

Invest in a set of serious rain gear. That way you will always be prepared for rain. And when you are prepared with a rain coat and rain pants, you know how it goes, you won't ever need them!

Winter Wear

If you ride horses in regions where winters get cold, you will forever be on the lookout for just the right warm coat, socks, and gloves to wear while riding. Don't rely on your snowmobile suit to ride. That would work fine just to clean stalls and work around the barn in the winter (although, unless it's below zero, you will probably get warm pretty fast doing barn chores in a snowmobile suit!). But if you wear a snowmobile suit while you're in the saddle, you might find yourself sliding off the other side in a matter of minutes. Again, a lot of winter wear is made specifically for horse riding. The extra advantage horse-specific apparel offers is that it's often warm without creating a lot of extra bulk.

Manufacturers of horse riding clothing make coats, ski pants, and all manner of cold-temperature riding clothing. If you are good at planning ahead, you could get the best deals buying your winter riding clothing in the early spring when tack shops and catalogers are trying to blow out their excess seasonal inventory.

Follow the advice given for any wintertime outdoor activity: Dress in layers. Thermal underwear (top and bottom) followed by cotton shirt and jeans, a thin sweater, a vest, and then an outer coat allow you to take layers off as you warm up (and before you perspire too much). You can also try the new polyester garments that wick away sweat, so you don't get as cold.

In the arena, you can throw things on the rail and retrieve them when you start to chill. If you are out on the trail, you might have to tie coat sleeves around your waist or to the back of your saddle.

Buy clothing that is made for horseback riding. It will be reinforced for wear and comfort in all the right places. It will stand up to the rigors of hours in the saddle: horseback riding is an activity not quite like any other. And riding clothing is made with safety around horses in mind— for example, good riding gear will not have cotton string pulls like those found on most hooded sweatshirts. If that string gets caught on any part of a moving horse, you could easily be choked.

Showing Off

This chapter has been limited to everyday riding—either out on the trail, in lessons, or schooling around the arena. If you get into showing horses, you will want to wear very specific clothing. Western pleasure riders wear very different show clothes compared with barrel racers who dress more casually for this fast-paced event. English riders dress completely differently, not only from Western-style riders but also from riders in different English events. Dressage riders dress more formally than stadium jumpers who dress more formally still than cross-country competitors. Check Chapter 16 for more specifics on the clothing expected in different types of competition.

Chapter 3

Tack

"Tack" is the general term used for the equipment involved with horseback riding. Technically it refers to equipment specifically for the horse. However, in tack shops and tack catalogs, you will find all the rider apparel and equipment you might need (and more) as well. This chapter covers what you need to know about riding equipment to get started.

Why Saddles Are Useful

The saddle is probably the most complex piece of equipment you will use or buy when it comes to riding. No matter what kind of saddle you use—English or Western, dressage or roping, endurance or barrel racing—the saddle serves two main purposes:

- To distribute the rider's weight across the horse's back evenly and away from the spine, and
- To help the rider maintain an appropriate position and to remain on the horse's back.

You can ride without a saddle—it's known as riding "bareback," and people do it all the time. While riding bareback is fun, it's not appropriate for a long ride for the comfort of both you and the horse. A short jaunt through the woods after a deep snowfall with the warmth of the horse's body right next to yours is nice. Some instructors have riders ride bareback for short stints to help them gain a better appreciation of the horse's movements and to help learn more about balance. But, for the most part, you want to ride with your horse saddled.

FACT

In the United States, if you go on a trail ride at a stable that specializes in conducting trail rides for any level of rider, you will almost exclusively see Western saddles in use. With more saddle area, they offer the novice rider more things to hang onto, and the rider can feel more secure in the saddle.

The Western Saddle

A Western-style saddle is so named because the saddle originated in the western part of the country, used by cowboys in the work they do on horseback. The Western saddle is substantial in size and can be substantial in weight.

Cowboys need a comfortable saddle for long hours on a horse. They also need space for lots of paraphernalia required to do their job—saddle bags, a lariat rope, hobble straps, maybe even a bedroll, some campfire tools, or a rifle. The saddle also needs to be extremely sturdy. Western saddles used for roping cattle have large horns—the protrusion at the front—that the cowboy, once he's roped a cow, can "dally" or tie-off to and hold the cow. Western-style saddles that won't be used for roping do not need such a big strong horn, but they still have a horn because it's integral to the style. However, the solely decorative horn can be much smaller.

Western saddles are typically used in disciplines such as barrel racing and other games in shows called "gymkhanas." They are used on reining horses (a type of competition whose roots come from ranching and cow working) and in general showing. Any class designated "Western" will require a Western-style saddle.

Stirrups come in several different styles. Some of the choice is simply personal preference, while certain styles are traditional for a certain kind of saddle. For instance, a barrel racing saddle often has narrow stirrups called "ox-bows" because they are sort of shaped like an ox bow.

Parts of a Western Saddle

The Western saddle has several parts:

- The **horn** is a vertical protrusion in the front of the saddle.
- The **seat** is sized for the human by taking a measurement diagonally.
- The **stirrups** are the equipment dangling down on either side that you set your feet on.
- The **fenders** are the wide pieces of leather that your legs rest against and that attach the stirrups to the main part of the saddle.
- The **tree** is a critical but invisible structure around which the saddle is built.

- The **pommel** is the hump in front of where you sit that the horn sticks out of.
- The **cantle** is the back of the seat. Some saddles come up from the seat and bend back in what is called a Cheyenne roll. Others just are straight.
- The **skirt** is the part under the seat that creates the base of the saddle that sits on the horse.
- The long strap of leather that hitches through the cinch to secure the saddle is called the **latigo**.
- The **back cinch** is found on most stock saddles and is useful for keeping the saddle down when the rider ropes a cow and dallies to the horn.
- A small strap of leather goes between the front and back cinch to keep the back cinch from slipping back too far into the horse's tender flank.

ALERT!

If you use a back cinch on a Western saddle, always be sure to buckle up the cinch keeper. This keeps the back cinch from traveling too far back into the sensitive loin area that, for some horses, can cause the back cinch to get called its other name, "bucking strap."

How to Put on a Saddle

English and Western saddles are quite a bit different to put on when it comes down to the specifics, but in general they have the same pieces. Here's how to put on a Western saddle:

1. Before you even think about picking the saddle up to put it on, be sure that all the parts are organized. Get the latigo wrapped up neatly on the left side cinch ring; tie or clip off the front and back cinch on the right side. Make sure the breast collar is neatly clipped to the saddle on either the right or left.

Photograph by Cheryl Kimball

▲ Whether you ride in an English saddle (left) or Western saddle (right), good horsemanship is basically the same.

2. Put your saddle blanket on. Adjust it a little forward so you can slide the whole thing back just a tiny bit in the direction of the hair once you have the saddle on. Besides, saddle blankets rarely slip forward while riding but they often slip back so starting more forward to begin with will help ensure your pad is always between the saddle and the withers.

3. Pick up the saddle on your right side. Put your arm across the seat and grab the right side of the cantle with your right hand. Rest the left side of the saddle on your right hip. If you can, hold the left front corner of the saddle with your left hand and use it for a little added oomph when you bring the saddle up.

4. Turn "potential energy" into "kinetic energy" (didn't know you'd need physics to ride, did you?) by moving the saddle slightly behind you and swinging it forward and up onto the horse's back.

5. Momentum will help swing the right stirrup to the other side, clearing the horse's back. Be careful not to swing so hard you swing the saddle right over the horse and onto the ground on the other side! That might

cause a jumpy horse to jump right in your direction. You will need to experiment with how much swing is enough, since it all depends on your height, the horse's height, and the weight of the saddle. This combination is different for everyone.

6. When the saddle is almost to the horse's back, ease off like you would the brake of your car if you came to a quick stop at a stop light, so the saddle eases onto the horse's back. Most horses will forgive you a slam or two onto their backs, but if this is your modus operandi, you will begin to have saddling problems as the horse anticipates that saddle slamming on top of him. Adjust the saddle and saddle pad as necessary.

7. Go around to the right side and take down the cinches. Go back around to the left and do up the *front* cinch first. Never do up the back cinch or breast collar first. They are not tight enough to hold the saddle on, and if the horse spooks, the saddle will turn but still be connected to him, and quite a wreck could ensue.

8. Buckle the back cinch, then the breast collar.

The English Saddle

English saddles are designed to do the same thing as a Western saddle—distribute the weight of the rider and give the rider a secure seat on the horse. English saddles are smaller than Western saddles. They are made of leather with the exception of some synthetic models that have been introduced over the past couple of decades.

English saddles are used for disciplines that require a lot more intense movement on the part of the horse—jumping, for instance. Some styles of riding use English saddles simply out of tradition—for instance, the movements of the horse known as dressage can certainly, for the most part, be done in a Western saddle as well as an English saddle. But you will not see a Western saddle in a dressage competition.

English saddles have most of the same parts as a Western saddle, with a few minor differences:

- English saddles have thin stirrup "leathers" not "fenders," with metal not leather stirrups hanging from them.

- The English saddle does not have a horn. This is one of the key differences between English and Western saddles, although they do have a raised pommel area in front of the seat.
- English saddles do not have "skirts," which gives them much less bulk and they are more suited for activities like jumping, foxhunting, and racing.

There are more distinct differences in styles of English saddles than Western styles. English saddles come in several different styles.

Dressage

Dressage style saddles, which often have a high cantle and a deep seat, seat the rider quite upright in the saddle with legs pretty straight.

Hunt seat

Hunter-style saddles have flaps (called fenders in the Western saddle) that are more rounded and forward than dressage style, allowing the rider to more easily get into jumping position. This style also has a shorter stirrup length.

All-Purpose

The all-purpose saddle is a cross between a hunt saddle and a dressage saddle. Some say that an all-purpose saddle is simply good at nothing; others find that they suit their needs perfectly—not too upright, not too forward, not too deep a seat but enough to feel secure.

Endurance Saddles

Endurance-style saddles come in both English styles and Western styles. They are designed for long-distance trail riding, and therefore the focus is on a high level of comfort for both horse and rider. Two features an endurance saddle include are lots of rings for clipping water bottles, sponges, and other on-the-trail needs and a crupper ring in the back and to use a piece of equipment called a crupper that wraps under the horse's tail and helps keep the saddle in place. Endurance saddles might have some seat selection for high comfort like gel-inserts or orthopedic foam.

FACT

Everything about horseback riding has been traditionally done from the left side—putting on the bridle, putting on the saddle, mounting, leading—a habit presumably having arisen because warriors carried swords. Getting your horse used to having things done on both sides can really help him feel more balanced. It can come in handy when you have to mount from a rock on a woodsy trail on the right side.

Saddle Fit

The stable will take care of saddle fit for their school horses if you are taking lessons. The next step after fitting the horse is to fit the saddle to you. Western saddles come in seat sizes for adults starting at around 14 inches for petite people and as much as 18 inches for larger seat sizes. English saddles run at larger sizes to begin with; smaller seats are around 16 inches and 18 inches is a fairly regular size.

Riding in a saddle that fits you is important. While it can be a half size or so off, any more than that is not good for more than a short ride. If you lease a horse, and the horse has its own saddle, be sure that saddle also fits you. You might find you need your own saddle anyway.

If you are acquiring a saddle for your own horse or one you are leasing, first, of course, you need to figure out what kind of saddle you want to ride in. While deciding, be sure to do some research on those saddles. There are many manufacturers of both English and Western saddles. Check online for possibilities, then plan to visit some tack shops. It's worthwhile to drive 100 miles or so to look at different kinds of saddles.

While at the tack shop, your first consideration is to be sure the saddle fits you. Wear riding boots so you can simulate as best as possible the way you will feel while in the saddle. Sit in it for a few minutes. Adjust the stirrups to the appropriate length.

To bring the saddle home, you essentially will need to purchase it—use a credit card if you can. If it doesn't fit your horse, you can return it, and they will simply credit your card (often with a small "restocking fee," so ask about that up front). You will need to be very careful when riding it—don't try it out when it's raining, for instance—but the shop or manufacturer encourages you to ride in it normally for up to a week. You can even conduct all this business through the mail, although it will cost you shipping fees (for Western saddles that can add up), and it's difficult to know up front if the saddle fits you, so you are taking more of a risk. However, the number of tack shops that stock the very best saddles is a bit limited, so sometimes shipping is the only way.

How do you tell that the saddle fits your horse? The manufacturer or the dealer should give you some specific instructions. In general, for a Western saddle, the weight should rest on the horse across the center part of the left and right edges of the saddle. The front should not pinch the horse's shoulders and should rest naturally right behind the edge of the shoulder blade. The back should not dig into the horse's loin area nor should it be so long on the horse that it interferes with the horse's hip movement. The horse will help you know if the saddle is especially uncomfortable. If you ride for a while and get the horse a little sweaty, carefully examine the hair under where the saddle pad was to look for dry spots (which can indicate excessive pressure) or odd-looking whorled hair or hair rubbed against the grain. Sometimes that can be caused by the saddle pad not sitting flat, so again, be sure to ride in the saddle a few times.

The Cost of a Saddle

When it comes to saddles, cheaper is definitely not better. That doesn't mean to say you need to spend several thousand dollars on a saddle. But do buy the very best saddle you can afford. Your body will thank you, and your horse will thank you. And if you do any significant amount of riding, a well-made saddle will definitely hold up much better than a cheaper one. Most saddle repairs are hard to make yourself, so a broken saddle means you might be out some riding time. And a poorly made saddle piece can break at an inconvenient and even dangerous moment.

Both English and Western saddles average anywhere between $500 on the very cheap side to $2,500 on the higher quality side. You can pay anywhere in between and definitely higher if you get a custom-made saddle with some special extras.

Keep in mind that a high-quality saddle holds its value extremely well. Take good care of your saddle. Five or ten years down the road, you can command almost as much as you paid for it if you sell it, especially since prices for new saddles will have gone up by then.

Saddle Blankets

You always want to use a saddle blanket under your saddle. A saddle blanket does help protect the horse's back a little, but a high-quality saddle should be completely comfortable without a saddle blanket. The blanket essentially keeps the underside of the saddle clean, and if you pick one that complements your horse's color, it looks nice.

Western saddles need blankets large enough to fit under the full length and width of the saddle. Wool Navajo blankets woven in interesting patterns and beautiful color schemes are standard fare for Western riding. Wool felt pads that come in different thicknesses and with different color canvas coverings are also used often.

Although lots of people do it, it's best not to bunch several blankets under the saddle. The best approach is to keep it simple. And keep your blankets clean. It's hard to wash a lot of horse stuff; the best approach with saddle blankets can be to take them to a hand car wash and power hose the underside to spray the hair and dried sweat off.

FACT

Buying used can be a very smart way to get a good saddle. Many tack shops have a used tack section. Online catalogs often list used equipment. Not only can you get a higher quality saddle for the amount of money you can afford, but it's already partially broken in, which when it comes to leather can be perfect. It takes a lot of riding to fully break in a saddle. If you are a part-time rider, a used saddle can be just the thing.

English saddle pads come either as pads that are in the shape of the saddle and barely stick out from underneath or dressage-type pads that are large and square and come in bright colors. Some "endurance pads" also come with pockets to put stuff in.

Bridles

The other essential item for riding that you will need is the bridle. Nonhorse people often confuse the bridle with the halter: the halter is a headpiece that is used to lead the horse around while a bridle is the headgear used to control a horse while riding it. A bridle consists of a bit and reins.

If a horse has been taught to cooperate, putting on a bridle is easy. There are many ways of doing it, but here's one:

1. Organize the reins and hang them over your left arm. Drape the crown of the bridle on your forearm with the bit facing toward your body.
2. Stand on the horse's left side and ask him to drop his head to your level. If he can't do this, you could spend some time teaching him to help you out.
3. Take the crown piece of the bridle in your right hand, gently bring the bit under the horse's chin, and pull the bridle up. Hold onto the forelock and the top of the bridle.
4. Drop the bit down and bring it up into the horse's mouth. But WAIT! If the horse has been taught to help you bridle him, he will open his mouth for the bit. But if he is young or he just waits for you to do everything, you might need to slip your thumb in the area in the side of his mouth between his incisors and his molars (where there are no teeth) to encourage him to open his mouth.
5. Gently slide the bit in.
6. Gently slip the right side of the bridle over his ear, all the time being careful not to be rough on the horse's right eye, which you can't see.
7. Gently slip the left side of the bridle over the left ear.
8. Buckle the cheek strap.
9. Check out both sides and adjust everything neatly.
10. Organize your reins.

Photograph by Cheryl Kimball

▲ When using a "double-rigged" Western saddle—both front and rear cinch—safe protocol is to always snug up the front cinch first. This way if the horse jumps, the saddle will stay in place.

Photograph by Cheryl Kimball

▲ Next, buckle the back cinch, which doesn't get tightened as much as the first and if done up alone would allow the saddle to slip under the horse's belly but not drop off, a recipe for disaster in most cases. There should always be a piece of leather to buckle between the two cinches so the back cinch doesn't end up in the horse's flank.

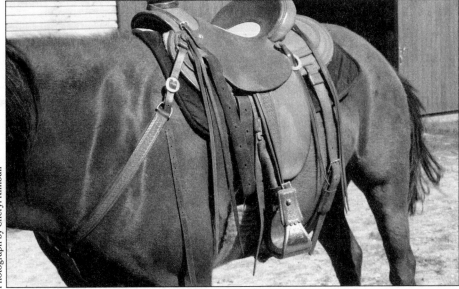

Photograph by Cheryl Kimball

▲ Finally, if your Western saddle has a breast collar, buckle that on last. And when you take the saddle off, do the opposite—undo the breast collar, then the back cinch, then the front cinch. Buckle cinches up to leather keepers on the off side and hook the breast collar to the off side rings so when you take the saddle off everything is snug in its place and ready for your next ride.

If the horse is evasive about having the bridle put on, don't blame the horse. Examine your own bridling technique. This is the horse's head—his muzzle is very sensitive; his vision is such that your hands are just a big blur to him; you are working around his sensitive ears; you are sticking a big cold piece of metal in his mouth. Be gentle, but be efficient, don't linger and tickle him. If he isn't happy about the bridling, try some different techniques to see if they help.

There are a few distinct parts of a bridle you need to know about.

The Headstall

This is the leather strapping that goes behind the horse's ears and cheek straps hang down either side of the cheeks. The headstall's sole purpose is to keep the bit in the horse's mouth. The parts of the headstall are the crown piece that goes behind the ears, the cheek straps, and the chin strap that wraps underneath the cheek and buckles.

The Bit

This is the piece of equipment that most people know about. The simplest bit is the snaffle bit, which is a straight piece of metal with a hinge in the middle. On either end are "rings." These rings can be round, O-rings, or have one flat side, known as "D-rings." The bridle's cheek pieces attach to the rings. More severe bits include "curb" bits that, instead of a hinged mouthpiece, have a solid metal mouthpiece with a high piece in the middle called a "port." The higher the port, the potentially harsher the bit. Bits can be made of iron or stainless steel. Sometimes copper pieces are inlaid in the bit, which are said to help the horse salivate and keep the bit lubricated. Like anything to do with riding, there are many incarnations of the bit.

FACT

No bit is harsh when used by a rider with "good hands." The experienced rider uses the bit as a communication piece, not as a weapon. But it takes years to have good hands. Potentially severe bits should be left to the experienced rider on well-schooled horses. If the communication between you and your horse is not going well, stay with or return to the snaffle bit. Ninety-five percent of all riders go in the wrong direction by using a more severe bit.

The Reins

The reins connect the bit to your hands, so that you can communicate with the horse. Even something as simple as reins have many different styles. "Split reins" are typically two separate leather straps, one coming from each ring of the bit. "Mecate reins" is a Spanish vaquero style of rein that is one long piece of mohair, parachute cord, or other kind of braided rope. They pass through the bit connected by leather straps called "slobber straps" and make a continuous rein; one end ties off on the left side and a long tail is left that can be used as a lead rope when you need to get off your horse to, say, doctor a cow. English reins are often leather straps that buckle together in the middle. Some reins are braided, some are smooth; for everyday riding, it depends on your preference. For horse shows, you need to know the appropriate style of reins for the discipline you are riding in.

ALERT!

Other Riding Equipment

The saddle and the bridle are the essential pieces of riding equipment for the horse. But if you like stuff, you have taken up the right hobby. A visit to any well-stocked tack shop will show you that the horseback riding world is filled with as much stuff as your heart desires.

You can certainly completely empty your wallet and stack up the charges to your credit card if you get carried away with buying horse-related stuff. Be sensible: buy what you need in the highest quality you can and purchase a few things for the sheer fun of it (hoof glitter? brightly colored sparkling bell boots?), but don't buy loads of stuff that you'll never, ever end up using. If you find yourself starting to buy items this way, quickly give them away or put them up for sale in the consignment section of a tack shop. Unused horse stuff simply accumulates dirt and dust. Keep some basic first aid supplies on hand and hope you never need to use them. But for everything else, if you don't use it over the course of a full year, let it go. And don't buy more!

Breast plate

Both English and Western saddles can be used with what is known as a breast plate or breast collar. This attaches to the saddle on either side and attaches through the front legs to the girth. It helps hold the saddle in place so that it does not slip too far back.

Protective Foot and Leg Wear

As a general rule, horses who have proper "conformation" (i.e., they are put together proportionally) and who have experience in mixed terrain do not need protective foot and leg covering. But a horse that has a conformation flaw in the leg or foot—toed out, toed in, a slightly crooked leg, or legs too close together—may need protective boots or leg wraps to prevent him from hurting himself or pulling a shoe off if he strikes one foot or leg with another foot. A horse that is used for activities like jumping, where he might strike a rail, needs protective leg wear, especially when he is just learning. A few raps to the front of the front leg, called the "canon bone," and the horse quickly will be discouraged about jumping. Some people put all manner of boots and leg wraps on a horse before hauling him in the trailer. This is mostly unnecessary, but you need to do what you are comfortable with. If the horse is new to trailering and has never had leg wraps on before, you should spend a lot of time getting him accustomed to them. Otherwise, you can cause more problems than you prevent.

Alternative Bridles

Several alternatives exist to the regular bridle. One is a bridle that does not have a bit but works off pressure to other parts of the horse's head, mostly the "poll," the area between the horse's ears. Another kind of bitless bridle is known as a sidepull; typically the reins can be attached so pressure can be applied to the poll area or just the sides of the horse's cheeks. A "trail bridle" has clips to hook the bit on so you can easily take the bit out of the horse's mouth and let the bridle double as a halter.

Tie Downs or Martingales

Both English and Western tack offer a piece of equipment commonly known as a "tie down." This piece of equipment often comes as part of a breast collar and attaches to the horse's bridle and between the horse's legs to the girth. They do exactly what they say—tie the horse's head down so he can't lift it above a certain level. Tie downs come in "running" style and "standing" style. The running style has rings that the reins go through and gives the horse a bit more freedom of movement than the standing style.

The tie down is a perfect example of a piece of equipment designed to be the quick and easy solution. Don't use this instead of taking the longer and harder route of learning good horsemanship so that you can help your horse not need to put his head up so high. Horses raise their heads high to avoid the pressure of the bit; in the case of the school horse that tolerates many different levels of rider and doesn't get to feel much in the way of consistency, the tie down is probably a useful tool. If you take lessons, you will run across this piece of equipment. But do not let anyone talk you into using it on your own horse. Instead find someone who is willing to help you learn how to better your horsemanship so your horse doesn't feel the need to escape the feel of your hands.

ALERT!

Don't resort to things like tie downs and tight nosebands to solve "problems" like a horse raising her head too high or playing with the bit. Any horse issue can be solved with good horsemanship; you just need to find the right teacher to help you. When you are riding other people's horses, such as in lessons or if you lease a horse, you will have to expect to use the kind of equipment they require. However, for your own horse, go the better horsemanship route.

Chapter 4

Riding Lessons

Who takes riding lessons? How do you find a barn that offers lessons, and how do you know whether it's the right place for you to learn? Are there different teaching styles? Will you need your own horse or equipment? This chapter will teach you how to find the lessons that are right for you.

Who Takes Lessons?

The recreational horseback riding scene has a few distinct types of riders. First are the kids. They are enthusiastic, absolutely adore horses, are flexible and resilient, and have a blast taking lessons. Most show little fear but even those kids who do seem a little fearful also seem eager to learn to jump, run barrels, and other high-energy horse activities. They love grooming and fussing over the horses, but most of all they want to get on and ride.

The adult scene seems typically full of two kinds of riders:

- Those who used to have horses and stopped horseback riding for a while, usually for some years.
- Those who have always dreamed of having a horse.

For either group, college, jobs, and raising a family usually have taken precedence for the past twenty or so years. Finally having a horse becomes their "doing something for myself" activity.

Photography by Kit Houghton

▲ Taking lessons is a great way to ride if you don't own a horse.

Occasionally couples get into riding together, but typically these riders are women in their late thirties and early forties. Riders of this demographic often go about horseback riding systematically, carefully planning every phase of their progression in the sport. Their main focus revolves around two concepts: have fun and be safe.

You might find yourself into horses because you finally gave in to your twelve-year-old daughter's plea to take lessons. That's great! Many a parent of a teenage daughter has been grateful that horses seem to be more important than boys—at least for a few years! Perhaps you are learning to ride and would really like your kids to take it up, too. Riding is a great family activity but don't force horseback riding on your child. If she is simply not interested, she isn't interested. It would be a shame to turn her off horses forever, especially if she is simply frightened of them.

Beginners and those returning to riding after years out of the saddle would do themselves and the horses they ride a favor by taking some lessons. Many people think that since they rode as a child they are still "experienced" riders. But horseback riding requires muscles that almost no other activity calls for; so if you haven't ridden in five, ten, or fifteen years, getting back into riding slowly is best for your body and for your horse.

Another factor to consider is that with increasing age comes an increasing sense of self-preservation. Children are usually fearless riders; adults are usually not. A frightening experience with horses can take an adult a long time to overcome. Feeling safe is an important element to enjoying horses and horseback riding. Your instructor, the barn the instructor operates out of, and the school horses the instructor uses must make you feel safe.

Riding instruction comes in many forms. At first, you might have no idea what specific type of riding you eventually will focus on. At this stage, it really doesn't matter whether you take English or Western riding lessons. The important thing is to get balanced and find your riding seat—basically learn how to be comfortable on a horse—either again or for the first time.

Lesson Barns

If you are a typical American and have more activities and duties to spend your time on than there are hours in a day, your search for a place to take riding lessons probably should begin with lesson barns that are easy to get to. If it's too much of a hassle to get to the lesson barn, you will find it difficult to get there regularly. And a regular riding time is very important when taking lessons.

Variety

Besides locale, you also want a barn where you feel comfortable. Some barns have set themselves up to be geared toward a specific discipline. They offer lessons only in that discipline, the barn is organized around only the kind of arenas and equipment that particular discipline requires (e.g., the only riding arena is a formal dressage ring or the indoor arena has jumps up everywhere). Everyone is always kitted out in the perfect outfit.

Maybe you know exactly what discipline you would like to ride in, and this kind of specification is okay with you. But if you are new to riding or just getting back into it, you probably don't really know yet what kind of riding you are interested in. Or you might think you know, but if nothing else is available, you won't get the opportunity to investigate the possibilities.

FACT

The Internet is, as usual, a useful tool in finding horseback riding instruction. Sites such as *www.horsebackridingstables.com* provide state-by-state listings for riding stables and a related site, *www.ridingacademies.com*, shows lesson barns. Of course, not all stables are listed but these Web sites are certainly a good start.

Finding a Barn

The first thing you can do to try to find a place to take lessons is look in the phone book. You can try looking under "horses." If there's nothing there, try Horseback Riding Academies or just Riding Academies.

If there is a tack shop in your area, it is probably the very best place to actively look for a riding stable that gives lessons. The tack shop personnel will have made it their business to know where all the large barns are located in their market area. They will know what type of riding each one focuses on so they can be sure to stock up on the kinds of equipment those riders might come looking for.

Don't call the tack shop, stop in. Try to go there during a time when they might not be particularly busy. Don't go just when the shop is closing. During nice riding weather, a weekend afternoon can be slow for tack shops since a lot of horse owners are off riding or at horse shows.

Horse shows are another place to look for stables that give lessons. Many lesson barns bring groups of students to horse shows. You can see who is working with students and in which disciplines. Stand along the fence rail and watch the show. If you are the type of person who can talk with anyone, chat with other people watching the show (although don't interfere with them trying to watch their child win a ribbon!).

Find out who the coaches are on the sidelines and what barns they are from. You can try to find out what the coach's reputation is as an instructor, but don't rely totally on these kind of opinions, just add it to your information gathering.

Certainly if someone has a jacket on with such-and-such stables written across the back, see if you can get a moment when they aren't busy to ask about their stable. Ask for a card. Anyone from a serious lesson barn probably will have a stack of business cards on hand.

Look for business cards posted in both tack shops and at the secretary's booth at horse shows. You will have to be a little bit of a detective in finding the best barn for you. Most of all, you want to feel like it's a place where you could enjoy being around horses.

Evaluating Lesson Barns

When you make that first call or visit, some things to consider are:

- Does the barn manager or owner make you feel comfortable, like she was happy you called?
- Did she act like she could spend time with you on the phone? Or at least arrange a phone appointment time when she could spend time with you?

- Was she breathing hard like she was giving a lesson while on the phone with you? (Not something you want to be happening if you are the student!)
- Was she willing to give the name of a student or two (or ask if the student would mind giving his name) so that you could ask about the lesson program there?
- Perhaps most important, did she say that it was okay for you to watch a lesson?
- Lastly, if she said she would get back to you, did she?

Now you are ready to get in the car and visit a couple of the barns you found in your search.

If you simply don't feel safe at a facility, go with your instincts and find somewhere else to take lessons or board your horse. Never do anything unsafe just because someone asks you to. It's one thing to be a little anxious about trying something new with your horse, it's quite another to feel unsafe. Remember, your instincts are often right.

Diving In

Sometimes it takes just diving in and starting lessons somewhere to find out what you like and don't like about a barn or what you are looking for in an instructor. Some lesson barns offer lessons at a per-lesson rate but give a discount if you pay up front for a set of five, six, or ten lessons. This multiple-lesson discount is great, but don't do it until after you take at least a couple of lessons and determine whether you enjoy this barn and instructor.

FACT

Riding lessons shouldn't be just about being in the saddle. Most stables will expect you to learn how to groom and tack your own horse properly and safely. Don't be afraid to speak up if you can't remember how to use some piece of equipment. There are lots of straps to do up and buckles to fasten when it comes to horse equipment—your safety and your horse's comfort depend on each one being done up properly. It takes some practice to get to the point where putting the saddle and bridle on come as naturally as tying your shoe.

Watching a Lesson

As mentioned earlier, any barn where you are considering taking lessons should welcome you to come watch a lesson. Although it's not necessary to watch an entire lesson, try to stay if you can. It will tell you a lot.

Arrive fifteen minutes or so before the lesson is scheduled to start and watch the lesson horse being tacked up. Sometimes students are allowed to tack their own horses, sometimes barn personnel tack the horse. It often depends on how much experience the student has.

Be mindful of a few things while watching a lesson: Does the lesson start on time? In other words, is the instructor respectful of the student's time? When you are dealing with live animals, it's difficult to keep time limits or predict everything; if something is happening in the previous lesson that makes it apparent why the lesson is running long, that is understandable. But if the instructor is chatting on the phone or just not efficient with time, you need to decide if you have the time and patience to take lessons there. Try to watch a beginner lesson if you can. An instructor will probably be a bit tougher on a more advanced student than someone just learning.

ESSENTIAL

Taking lessons at an active horse facility gives you a chance to experience horseback riding without purchasing much of anything except the lesson itself. You will need a pair of good jeans (or breeches for English riding) and some sort of sturdy boot with a heel. You'll eventually want your own helmet, but until you know you are really interested, you'll do fine using the facility's equipment for things that are specific only to horseback riding—a helmet, the horse, and all the tack.

Do students look like they are enjoying the lesson? Does the instructor have a good rapport with the students? The lesson doesn't have to be a stand-up comedy act, but by the time the lesson ends, students certainly should seem like they had fun and are eager to come back for the next lesson.

Sometimes a lesson goes awry for any number of reasons that have nothing to do with the instructor. If you like a place or an instructor overall but the specific lesson you watch doesn't suit you, try coming back another time and watching a different lesson.

Group or Individual Lessons?

You might have a preference whether you take private lessons where you are the only student or whether you join a group lesson. If you are a total beginner, you might want to take a few individual lessons and then join an existing group.

Individual lessons are usually a half hour to an hour long. If you haven't ridden for a long time, consider starting out with a half-hour lesson. This way you can slowly build up the muscles needed for riding. If you go for the hour lesson immediately, you might find yourself sore toward the end of the first lesson and definitely the next morning. Although it's kind of nice to know you've actually done something, you don't want to be so distracted by the pain that you can't learn anything or you dread going to your next lesson.

Once you've done a few half-hour lessons, increase to an hour if you can. At what point you do that is up to you. Be sure to talk with the instructor up front about this kind of progression; she can plan your lessons accordingly and think about the best horses for you to ride.

FACT

There are a couple of organizations that will certify riding instructors. One is the American Riding Instructors Association (*www.riding-instructor. com*) and another is the Certified Horsemanship Association (*www. cha-ahse.org*). Riding instructors are not required to belong to either of these or any licensing or certifying association; membership is completely voluntary (except in Massachusetts), and there are many excellent long-time teachers who are not members. Certification does not guarantee that someone is an excellent teacher but it does indicate someone who cares about safety and student success.

Once you've had a few hour-long lessons, see if there is a group lesson you can join. Group lessons can be lots of fun. They usually go for a longer period of time than individual lessons, and they are usually cheaper, with the cost being divided up by the group. Groups can be formed around one discipline or just general riding. Four to eight riders makes a good number for a group; more than that, and the instructor has too many students to keep track of. Finding group lessons could require going to a larger facility that has enough school horses for everyone in the group. Depending on how much time and money you want to put into learning to ride, you could benefit from having an individual lesson every once in a while—maybe once every other week—even while you are taking group lessons.

Safety First

Safety should be a priority at any lesson barn. You can begin to assess the importance of safety at a facility the minute you begin to drive down the driveway. How do the fences look—in disrepair or neat and well constructed? Is there junk around the entrance to the barn—hoses, tools, an old stock tank that hasn't seen use in quite a while? Or is the entrance neatly manicured and free of obstacles that are potentially dangerous to both horse and human?

The Signs

Other signs of safety-first are actual signs. Almost every state in America has a limited liability act (LLA) for horseback riding facilities: each state's LLA reads a little differently, but the LLA basically states that you understand that horseback riding is inherently dangerous and you accept those inherent risks.

In most states, barn owners can buy signs stating the LLA to put up in a prominent place in their barn. Other signs you might see in a safety-oriented facility are ones that indicate wearing a helmet while mounted is a requirement, that appropriate footwear is expected when on the premises, and that children and dogs are to be kept under the control of their parents and owners, respectively.

Smaller signs like ones that indicate where things go, not to hand feed the horses, and "if you open it, shut it" kinds of instructions indicate that the barn owners care that things are put back in proper (and safe) storage and that they care about what kind of activity takes place at their facility.

Stick to the Rules

Not only do you want to see that the barn has signs up, but it should be apparent that the policies of those signs are adhered to. Maybe the barn policy clearly states "no loose dogs except for those belonging to the farm," but you notice that three of the boarders have brought their dogs and that the dogs are running around while a lesson is taking place. This is a small infraction, perhaps all three have permission from the barn owner or manager, and maybe you even like the idea of a bunch of dogs around. But every small erosion of the safety rules makes the place just a little less safe.

ALERT!

Be prepared to sign a "release form" wherever you take lessons. This form typically states that you understand that riding horses is dangerous and that you will not hold the facility liable if an accident happens.

Equipment

If you are seriously considering a particular barn, look at its tack room. Browse the tack room, if that's okay with the management, or look at tack while you watch a lesson. Gear used for giving lessons gets hard use, and keeping it clean and in good repair is critical. Here are things to look for:

- Are pieces of equipment dangling, held together with baling twine, or, worse still, breaking while a student is riding?
- Do the saddles and bridles have all their components?
- Does the tack look like it is cleaned regularly?

A private barn is a private matter; you can do anything you want if your barn is on your own property, and you have only your own horses in it. But when someone opens their barn up to the public and takes money for services, the barn should be prepared to make the place safe and presentable. That's the kind of barn where you want to take instruction.

The Horses You'll Learn On

To have a viable business, lesson barns need several horses known as "school horses." These are typically older horses that have experience being ridden by several different people. School horses need to be patient while riders pull on the reins, lose their balance, and bounce around on their backs.

Happy Horses

Walk through the barn aisle. What are the horses like where you are considering starting lessons? Even if you don't yet have much experience with horses, you can probably tell when an animal is content or on edge. If the horses are in their stalls, are they contentedly munching on hay? Or are they pacing around and snarling at passers-by? Horses that are not giving lessons that day should be outside getting fresh air and sunshine and frolicking with their buddies.

When you watch a horse being tacked up for a lesson, are the handlers smooth with the horse, gently and efficiently putting the gear on? Is the horse standing patiently, or is he frustrated and grouchy about being tacked up?

ALERT!

The natural environment for a horse is outside, roaming several miles a day and eating a little at a time all day long. Horses locked in stalls many hours of the day often develop habits known as "stable vices." These habits typically come from boredom and claustrophobia. Some weave back and forth endlessly at the stall door, some grip their teeth on the edge of a board and suck in wind, some paw. Some of these habits can be dangerous to the handler. A well-managed lesson barn keeps horses booked with lessons or outside frolicking with friends.

Changing Horses

You probably won't always ride the same horse for every lesson. The instructor might move you up to a more lively mount as you gain experience. You might get attached to a certain horse and be reluctant to try a new one.

Riding many different horses is the fastest way to get to be a better rider. But if there is a horse that makes you feel very safe, and you are learning well on him, ask your instructor if you can stick with him for a few more lessons. But be open to a change at some point, because you might be surprised at what you are ready for.

Your Own Horse

Perhaps you have your own horse. We'll discuss that more in Chapter 6. You might want to ride your own horse for lessons.

If you keep your horse at your home, some instructors might be willing to come to you, especially if they don't have their own facility. However, you will need to have an appropriate riding area to have a lesson. If you have a trailer, you can bring your horse to a facility that is open to giving you lessons on your own horse (liability issues can get in the way of that at some barns).

You might board your horse at a barn that gives lessons. That can be ideal; presumably if you like the barn enough to board your horse there, you will probably like their lesson program too.

The Right Instructor

People all learn differently. You need to understand a little about your own learning style to find the right instructor for you. Most people who are doing something for fun do not want to be yelled at and drilled like they are in the army. Find someone who is able to mix making the lessons fun with seriously teaching you good horsemanship.

Depending on your riding goals, how advanced your instructor is in his or her own riding career might not matter. To be able to eventually take your riding to the show ring, you want an instructor who has shown or is still actively showing horses.

At first, even if you do think you might like to show, whether your instructor has shown horses might not matter at all. You can learn a lot from someone who simply has been riding for a long time. Once you get the basics down and have some hours under your seat, you might want to think about finding an instructor who can be as much a coach as an instructor.

The Riding Coach

A riding coach can help you learn not only to ride in the discipline you want to progress in but also about the proper clothing for you and tack for your horse. You will need someone who can tell you about saluting to the judge (in dressage) or at what level the horse's head and neck should be in Western pleasure events and even about things like etiquette in the show ring.

Many barns have active show lessons and include shows at the barn—either private for just the students or open to the riding public. Some barns offer coaches who will take students on the road to shows and other competitive events like judged trail rides or gymkhanas.

Horse Clinics

Horse clinics have become a popular way of learning about horses in the past decade or two. Clinics are typically set up so that you need to bring your own horse. Many of them are not for total beginners but some are less overwhelming than others. And some clinics are more comprehensive with several classes offering something for everyone, from beginners to more advanced riders.

▶ Horse clinics have become so popular that you can find one nearby on almost any topic.

Photograph by Matthew Roberts

The best way to figure out if a clinic or particular clinician is right for you is to attend a few as an "auditor." For between ten to twenty-five dollars for the day, you can watch the entire clinic. Bring a chair, sunscreen, a hat, layers of clothing, drinks, snacks, and a lunch, and set up shop for the day. Don't spend the whole time talking and miss the clinic (and annoying other spectators) but do chat with a few people about their impressions. You will probably find spectators who have ridden with the clinician before or who are in another class that day; they will have some good insights into why they like the particular teacher.

Many facilities have the same clinicians back year after year—sometimes several times a year—so if you see someone you like, you'll have the opportunity to sign up for next time. Some clinicians become so popular at a facility, you might need to get your name in for the next time on the same day you watch the clinic. Be prepared to put a deposit down to reserve your spot.

Photograph by Cheryl Kimball

◀ These riders are taking a group horsemanship lesson at a clinic. Learning in a group allows you to work on things that are hard to do alone, such as the "weaving" exercise here, where every other rider rides in the opposite direction and goes to the left then right of each rider they meet.

Clinics are offered in almost every discipline imaginable as well as clinics that deal with general horsemanship, including handling the horse from the ground. Your needs and interests will change as you get more into riding.

To find clinics, check out your regional horse publication. Most have a list of events coming up in the next month, and many offer an annual calendar of events, typically at the beginning of the riding/showing season, usually in March.

The best way to find anything in the horse world—an instructor, a lesson barn, a horse, a boarding barn, a horse trailer, you name it—is to get out and talk with everyone horse-related whom you can find. Go to tack shops, horse shows, audit clinics, talk with the people in the horse barn at the local fairs. Use all the information you gather to make an informed decision about where to take lessons.

Relax!

Don't get overwhelmed with feeling you need to decide immediately what you want to do with the rest of your horseback riding life! If you are new to riding, just get riding at the best facility you can find that is convenient and comfortable. Attend shows and dressage tests and gymkhanas. Talk with other riders at the barn or at the shows. Talk with your instructor. (Good instructors will not lead you only toward the style of riding they teach; good instructors want students who are enjoying what they are learning.) You will not ruin your horseback riding future by simply taking lessons in whatever style of riding the local barn offers while you sort out what you might like to do with this new adventure you've started on!

Chapter 5

Fitness Considerations

One of the significant benefits of becoming involved with horses is increasing your physical fitness. Riders derive health benefits such as better aerobic capacity and stronger muscles. And for those who are lacking in all aspects of physical fitness—ideal weight, aerobic capacity, as well as strength and muscle tone—getting involved with equestrian sports can be the ticket to better health.

Strength

You do not need to be unusually strong to ride horses—a petite seven-year-old girl can ride as well as a thirty-five-year-old man. Riding well-schooled horses and continually improving your own horsemanship will show you that overpowering a horse with your strength is unnecessary and should never be your goal. However, horseback riding is physical, and even for the day-to-day riding experience, you need some basic level of strength and muscle tone. For example, if you ride Western, putting a Western saddle on smoothly requires some level of arm strength. For shorter riders, that can mean getting the saddle to a point above the level of your shoulders. Learning to swing the saddle back and using the energy to create momentum can help, but ultimately you have to have enough strength to swing the saddle back to begin with.

Just getting up on the horse can require some leg strength.

FACT

Horses that were bred to pull are called "draft horses." They are usually large in both height and breadth. In the United States, we have moved into an age where almost none of these horses are used for work such as plowing fields, forestry work, or pulling wagons. However, people have begun to find them enjoyable to ride. Draft horses tend to be pretty mellow (although everything about a horse can depend on how it's cared for). Draft horses crossed with "light" horses (also called riding or saddle horses) are becoming incredibly popular for riding.

Basically, you don't need to get into bodybuilding, but it helps to do some simple weight training. A moderate program of lifting hand weights of 3 to 5 pounds each three times a week can help a lot. Work various muscle groups—biceps, triceps, and shoulder muscles. A home weight bench is pretty inexpensive—if you have the room to set one up, a weight bench could allow you to work both upper and lower body muscles more easily.

Unless you are really out of shape, there isn't really any reason to hire a personal trainer and spend hours in the gym. Most horseback riders find it hard enough to fit in trips to the barn not to mention adding trips to the gym. If you want to go to the gym, that's great. Do enough to make a difference, but keeping your exercise routine simple enough so that you will follow through is a fine approach.

Body Movement

Besides a minor amount of strength and muscle tone, one of the first things you will learn as you begin to ride is how important it is to be able to move your body in certain ways and how you feel when you realize that you can't! "Independent movement" is extremely important to be a successful rider. As you ride around her in the ring, your instructor will be telling you to move your arm, your leg, drop your heel, move your pelvis, or raise your head. You will need to be able to move these body parts without moving other body parts—in other words, you will need to be able to move them independently.

Your instructor isn't asking you to do these things just to get a kick out of playing a little game of Simon Says and seeing how well you do. The first thing your lesson instructor will work on is trying to help you get balanced on the horse—something called "finding your seat." To be balanced on a horse, you should be able to drop a plumb line from your shoulder and have your shoulder, hip, and ankle lie in a direct vertical line. So your first lessons—perhaps your first year or more of lessons!—will focus a lot on teaching you how to line these parts up. (Although this sounds like a rigid posture, you also don't want to be stiff.)

There are some movement therapies that horseback riders have come to embrace as being especially helpful to the equestrian.

ALERT!

Hand feeding horses, however entertaining, can set a dangerous precedent. While there are some horses that can be completely polite about it, most times you create a situation where the horse is always grabbing your pocket or sniffing at your hand. This could lead to biting—and a horse's jaw can exert enough pressure that he can bite off a finger in one bite. If you want to give horses treats, it's best to put the treat in their feed bucket and forget about feeding them by hand.

Yoga

These days most people are at least somewhat familiar with yoga. Practicing yoga has several benefits to the rider—it helps maintain a positive and peaceful mental state, which is always a good state to be in when working with horses. It helps extend your flexibility. Yoga practice can allow you to begin to understand and achieve this idea of independent movement. And yoga helps you simply become more aware of how your body operates and what you can do to impact movement.

Feldenkrais Movement Therapy

Over the course of his lifetime, a man named Moshe Feldenkrais developed thousands of exercises called Awareness through Movement (ATMs), which serve to help people understand movement of their bodies and become more aware of their control over that movement. ATMs can take from around thirty to forty-five minutes. The intention is to do them slowly and keep the movements simple and easy. The positive impact on your body's movement is remarkable and the impact on your riding can be dramatic.

The other component of Feldenkrais therapy is individual sessions with a certified practitioner. This is a hands-on therapy and the practitioner can help loosen up areas of your body that are a particular problem for you, such as pelvic tightness or upper body movement.

Finding Feldenkrais groups in remote areas can be difficult, but if you live in a major metropolitan area, you might be surprised to learn how much Feldenkrais movement therapy there is going on. To find out what's up near you, check the Feldenkrais Guild Web site for a list of practitioners in your area.

The Alexander Technique

The Alexander Technique offers a way to "rethink" the movements you make in your everyday activities. It helps you improve ease and freedom of movement to release tension and find balance. It's useful not only for horseback riding but for anything you do—from walking to sleeping to playing. You can see that it's quite similar to the Feldenkrais Method. Both are movement therapies designed to help you become more aware of your own body and its natural movement. The added benefit these methods have for the horseback rider is that the concept of "awareness" is critical in good horsemanship. Everyone who works with horses, whether it's horseback or on the ground, needs to constantly seek to improve their awareness level to improve their horsemanship. With perhaps a few selected individuals as exceptions, humans will never achieve the awareness level of horses, so the desire to improve our awareness level should never end.

Although both the Feldenkrais Method and Alexander Technique are used as a type of physical therapy to relieve specific pain, this is far from their only benefit. Anyone can benefit from learning and applying these techniques. It will improve everything about your daily life from sitting to sleeping to walking. Because they are very low-impact methods based on working within the ability of your specific body, both of these techniques are perfect for anyone at any age. Older people will become more pain-free in their movement and younger people will age with better movement ability than they might otherwise.

FACT

Health insurance providers occasionally consider penalizing horseback riders and others who pursue what they think of as dangerous sports, such as skiing, with higher premiums or even denial of coverage. But there is ample evidence to suggest that horseback riders are healthier and fitter than someone who spends the same amount of time watching television.

Pilates

The Pilates Method was created by Joseph Pilates. It uses exercise equipment to teach controlled movements that require concentration of mind and body. It's typically done under the supervision of trained teachers. Pilates can be very helpful for horseback riders.

Because Pilates requires special equipment you probably would want to find a Pilates studio and work with an experienced Pilates teacher. This shouldn't be too difficult to find almost anywhere in the country since

Pilates, although developed in the 1920s, has become extremely popular in the past few years.

Tai Chi

Any of the martial arts can be useful for horseback riders, but Tai Chi is especially pertinent. Tai Chi involves slow, balanced movement and can be incredibly useful in helping riders to gain balance.

Tai Chi is described as "moving meditation." Going slow and being relaxed is fundamental to this ancient practice. The intention is to work with the body and the mind simultaneously. Take a class or get a book to learn how to do the different movements and exercises of Tai Chi, such as "painting the wall" or "swimming on land." It's easy and gentle and suitable for anyone.

ALERT!

Any time you start a new exercise regimen, you should be sure you have had a recent general physical exam by your doctor. Being around horses always involves a certain amount of heavy lifting and activity you might not be accustomed to. Have your vital signs checked and get an all-around good bill of health. Be sure to tell your doctor you are getting involved with horseback riding so she or he knows the extent of physical activity you might be doing.

Flexibility

Being flexible is critical to riding. While it's important to maintain an upright posture, you also need to be fluid and relaxed—all at the same time. No one said horseback riding was easy! Don't worry, you don't need to bend like an Olympic gymnast. But there are several fundamental movements involved with basic horseback riding that require the rider to be a bit flexible.

One is simply getting on. If you are short and the horse you are riding is tall, you will want to use a mounting block. Mounting blocks are sold that are specific to horseback riding, and most barns have one or two scattered around the riding areas (some things, like an upside down milk crate, can work just as well). You can lead your horse near a portable mounting block and pick it up and move it over to the best position for getting on. That's one way. If you spend time teaching your horse to move his feet in any direction you ask, your mounting block doesn't have to be moveable. In that case, you could use just about anything for a mounting block—a fence rail, a big stump or rock out on the trail, a hump on the ground, a tire, a hay wagon, you name it—and you can direct your horse to position himself exactly beside the mounting block. The point is that no matter how flexible you are, your horse is big, and you are small. Don't drag yourself up there like a monkey unless you have no alternative.

But if the height of your horse is well proportioned with your height, you want to be flexible enough to get on from the ground. Unless you are tall and riding a pony (a combination not really recommended), this takes considerable flexibility of your legs to step up into the stirrup with the other foot still on the ground. And then you need to be able to reach one arm up in front of the saddle and one arm around the back side of the saddle to hoist yourself up (a little bounce on the foot on the ground helps get you started).This flexibility can be achieved through activities like yoga and tai chi and the other exercises mentioned above. But pre-ride basic stretching is also important.

Stretching

Typically, you want to warm your muscles up before you start stretching exercises. Jumping up and down, bouncing side to side, and running in place will help ready your muscles for some mild stretching. If you stretch with cold muscles, it will actually work against you because the muscle will be stretched against its will, and the body tells the muscle to contract against the pain, even if you don't feel any direct pain. So warm up your muscles first.

Then do some simple stretches. The area behind the calves called the hamstrings are important for a secure seat. Sitting down deep in the saddle and getting your heels down depends a lot on the flexibility of the hamstrings. Here's the classic hamstring exercise:

- Stand a little less than arm's length away from a wall.
- Put your hands flat on the wall for support, but don't lean your weight into them.

- Keep one leg straight and move the other foot out behind, but close enough so that your foot can remain flat.
- Bend the knee of the straight leg, and feel the hamstring on the other leg pull. DON'T BOUNCE.

Never stretch to the point of pain. Again, once your muscles feel pain they will contract to protect themselves, so by stretching until you feel pain, you are actually defeating your purpose.

Flexible Everywhere

The other area where it's important to be flexible specifically for riding is the pelvic area. The adductor muscles—the ones on the inside of your upper legs that bring your legs together—are very tight in most people. These muscles truly need to be stretched to avoid extreme discomfort, not only after a ride, but even a short time into a ride. Yoga and Feldenkrais can be a great help in getting these muscles more flexible. People who can easily and comfortably sit cross-legged with their feet interlocked have little problem with adductor muscles. Look for some simple stretches that target the adductors.

Riding requires you to be moderately flexible all over. Just because you sit on the horse and wrap your legs around the horse's barrel doesn't mean that your upper body should be ignored. In fact, the upper body is quite important. A couple of stretches that help out your torso, neck, shoulders, and rib cage area would prove useful. Essentially, you can never be too flexible. Stiffness anywhere always works against you in riding but you don't need to become a Gumby doll to be a great rider.

Give up the old notion that you should stretch your muscles to the point of feeling pain. When your muscles feel pulled more than they can comfortably stretch, they actually begin to contract to protect themselves. Your stretching regimen should consist of regular stretching exercises throughout the week along with some specific stretches—hamstrings, adductors, and upper body—right before riding.

Weight Maintenance

People who are overweight get fatigued faster than people who are a good weight for their height and body type. Fatigue is never good when it comes to horseback riding.

Rider weight can be an issue for the horse as well. A rider who is considerably overweight can create chronic back pain and leg pain in a horse they ride a lot. Again, this is not to say if you are overweight you can't ride—quite the contrary. Riding will be the best thing you ever came across! If your excess weight causes you to become fatigued more easily, imagine how great it is to have an outdoor activity you can do where the horse does a lot of the hard work for you. Overweight riders need to choose appropriately sized horses. Depending on the size of the rider—both weight and height—the best horse could be a draft horse or a horse that is half draft horse.

Riding itself won't cause you to lose weight. But enjoying riding and being around horses might provide a meaningful incentive to figure out how to reduce your weight, and therefore would be a great health benefit indirectly.

ALERT!

Some lesson barns and trail riding stables have a rider weight limit. Many of them simply don't have horses that are of appropriate size to carry a large rider—whether you are overweight or big and tall. If you are a plus-size and are interested in lessons or planning to go on a trail ride, call ahead to make sure they have a horse that is appropriate for you.

The Importance of Breathing

When you do yoga, you are constantly reminded of the importance of breathing. Breathing deeply helps the body get appropriately oxygenated. It also helps to calm and relax you. And breathing consciously helps stabilize you and keeps you from being rigid. All of these are important to good riding.

If you pay attention to learning good breathing habits on the ground, you will be more likely to breathe well automatically while in the saddle.

Breathing deeply while riding will help you relax, if you are a bit nervous. And it will help bring your balance right where it needs to be to stabilize your seat. If you find yourself bouncing around in the saddle, draw your attention to your breathing. You will probably find that you are holding your breath. Take in some deep breaths, and you should start to sink a little deeper into the saddle.

Good breathing techniques require you to have a flexible rib cage, and in turn can help your rib cage become more flexible. This is important to riding when, for instance, you need to turn your upper body (such as to look at an upcoming jump that is off to the side) without changing your seat position. Or to look at your instructor as she reminds you for the millionth time to "breathe"!

Mental Fitness

Riding horses also helps with mental and emotional fitness—a benefit that should not be underestimated. If you enjoy animals, the pleasure you can get from grooming a horse or riding through the woods is unmatched. The thrill of jumping over a jump or racing barrels can be just the right amount of excitement to perk up your otherwise routine life. Riding a precise dressage course or a reining pattern can provide an incredible sense of accomplishment and self-esteem. Just learning how to teach a horse something like setting himself up to stand just right to be judged at halter or to stand patiently for the horseshoer can be a very gratifying experience.

FACT

Studies about the benefits of riding horses have proven that being near such a large, beautiful animal, the movement of the horse, and consequential movement of the rider releases so-called "feel good" hormones called endorphins. The therapeutic benefits of riding have become so well documented that "therapeutic riding" has become a viable activity of the equine industry. Physical and emotionally handicapped people use riding to gain confidence, self-esteem, and to generally feel well.

Horses are big. Being comfortable around such a large animal brings most people a lot of satisfaction. Horses are very appreciative when treated fairly and in a way that considers their nature.

A bad day at the office can be turned around by an evening at the barn. There is something completely peaceful about the sound of a barn full of horses munching grain and hay. Even mucking stalls—a job that most nonhorse people find distasteful—can help calm you down after even the most frustrating day. And the simple fact of coming home from the barn exhausted will give even insomniacs a good night's sleep.

Horse Fitness

When it comes to fitness, the horse can't be ignored. If you are riding lesson horses exclusively, the general fitness of your horse will be taken care of by the regular riding that the horse gets giving lessons. If you ride your own horse or are leasing a horse, and you are its only rider, the sole responsibility for the horse's fitness lies with you.

Like the human body, the horse's body needs to be gradually built up to increasing levels of fitness for riding. Any horse in general good health and that isn't exceptionally young or exceptionally old can easily stand a one-hour trail ride on fairly level ground with mostly walking, a little bit of trotting, and maybe even a short sprint or two of cantering. But if your plans are for longer rides, intense trails with hills or even mountainous terrain, or lots of trotting and cantering, you need to help your horse build up to that level of activity both physically and aerobically.

If the horse you are riding spends most of his time in a box stall (hopefully not!), your job of increasing his fitness level is tougher and even more important. If your horse is out 24/7 and gets to move around in a large area and even play and run around with other horses, he will start at a higher level of physical fitness than the stall-bound horse.

So Goes the Horse

The rules are the same for the horse as the human. Take things slowly, gradually increase your riding time, and find exercises and riding opportunities that focus on the aspect of fitness that is most important for the kind of riding you intend to do. If you want to do some long-distance trail riding, for instance, work toward longer trail rides and increase your trotting time with each ride. Trotting and walking up hills will increase your horse's aerobic capacity, allowing him to carry you for a longer time and over more difficult terrain without having to overexert himself.

Pre-Ride

Like you, your horse could benefit from mild and brief stretches, particularly if the horse is older (upper teens), or if he stands around in a confined space most of the day. If your horse was trained well, he would have been taught to be flexible and not braced from the beginning. This early training would help him be more fluid for the rest of his life.

After you cinch up the saddle, one simple stretch is to stretch the horse's front legs out straight in front of him one at a time. Stretch him gently, supporting the leg with both hands. Don't force the leg straight, stretch as far as you can gently.

Another, more complex, stretch with many benefits gets the horse to bend his neck with greater ease. With a halter and lead rope on your horse, stand beside him just behind his shoulder blade, facing front. Pick up on the lead rope and ask your horse to bend his head back to you—you want him to turn his head straight, not bring his chin up. Go only as far as the horse is comfortable; when you feel no pressure at all—i.e., the horse is not bracing back against the halter—release your hold. Your goal is for the horse to keep his head in that position even though you've released the lead, not to snap his head back to normal position. Each time you do this, your horse will probably bend a little farther.

Always be aware of your horse's expression and response in doing these kinds of stretches. Never put yourself in dangerous positions, like directly in front of or behind the horse.

Practitioners

As a horse owner, you should look for a large animal veterinarian whom you can work with. The vet should become familiar with your horse and what you do with him.

Other practitioners could help your horse reach a higher level of fitness. Everything that can be done in people medicine can be done with animals—but until the past decade or so, medical treatments such as chiropractic and acupuncture services were considered too expensive and extreme. People were not willing to pay for them, so veterinary offices did not acquire the equipment needed or offer the service. This has changed, and you can get chiropractic and acupuncture services for your horse. Physical therapy is available, including hydrotherapy in which the horse walks down a ramp into a large swimming pool. If it can be done with humans, it can probably be done with your horse; whether you want to go to those extremes is up to you—and the size of your wallet. Most of a horse's physical fitness needs can be taken care of by conscientious and regular riding, turnout, and nutrition.

ESSENTIAL

When working with practitioners such as chiropractors or massage therapists, for either you or your horse, don't expect everything to be changed in one session. These kinds of manipulation therapies often take several sessions when beginning and then regular maintenance visits once or twice a year.

In general, just being around a barn involves physical activity on all levels. Mucking stalls, sweeping aisles, lifting hay bales, lots of walking, pushing heavy wheelbarrows—strength, flexibility, and aerobics, it's all needed here. Horses and horseback riding require you to attain some level of fitness. And the more you enjoy riding, the more motivation you have to do what it takes to ride well. It's really a win-win activity.

Chapter 6

A Horse Is a Horse?

If you are going to take horseback riding lessons you will need a horse to take them on. There are a few things you can do "unmounted" but ultimately—no horse, no horseback riding. But every horse isn't the same. A good instructor will help make sure you are properly mounted—on a horse safe enough for your level of horsemanship but also one that will help challenge you and increase your horsemanship skill.

The Lesson Horse

Perhaps you have decided to go to a lesson barn and take some lessons. Finding a horse in that case will be easy—a stable that gives lessons regularly will have at least one "lesson horse," preferably more, that they use specifically to give lessons.

What Makes a "Lesson Horse"?

A horse used for giving lessons is often referred to as a "lesson horse" or a "school horse." For the beginner, the perfect school horse has been exposed to a lot of different people and activities and has become mostly unflappable. A beginner needs to learn to be comfortable in the saddle and gain balance and stability on top of a horse. To do this, you don't need a horse that jumps and bolts at every dried leaf blowing across the arena floor. On a horse like that, the beginning rider will be easily unseated and will never gain confidence.

The more advanced rider will want a lesson horse schooled to a relatively high level in the discipline the rider is learning. Preferably, the horse's education is a level or two beyond the rider's desired level. The horse with the appropriate amount of education for the task he is being asked to do will perform with ease. The learner feels the movement without the horse having to rely too much on the rider to guide him.

FACT

Horse height is measured in a unit called a "hand." A hand equals 4 inches. A mature horse under 14.2 hands (or 58 inches) is considered pony size. (A "pony" is a specific breed, not just a small size.) A horse 14.2 hands and higher is a horse. Some breeds, such as the various types of "warmbloods" and thoroughbreds, tend to be very tall. Quarter horses and other stock-type horses tend toward around 15 hands.

The Good and Bad of Dullness

Horses have an incredibly high level of sensitivity. They had to be sensitive to survive in their natural environment; they needed to be always on alert, aware of predators, and everything else in their surroundings. A horse's body is set up for alertness. For example, its ears have large "pinnae" (the part that we can see) that swivel almost 360 degrees. In addition, the horse's eyes are set far apart on his head so the horse can see a wide range on either side while his head is down in the grazing position.

Humans start to dull the horse's sensitivity almost the instant we begin to interact with them. Advanced riders do not want the horse they are riding to be dull. Good horsemen and horsewomen work hard to learn how to retain the horse's sensitivity.

But the beginning rider can use a little dullness. The horse that makes a good beginner's lesson horse has learned to block out a lot of distractions. The beginning rider is often giving the horse mixed and confusing messages. The beginning rider often bounces around a lot when trying to learn to sit the trot or rock with the canter. A horse can feel a fly land on his rump—so you can imagine that a horse that has been ridden only by expert riders in a way that retains that innate sensitivity will have a hard time with a beginning rider bouncing around.

Perhaps the perfect example of dullness are the horses that you ride out on a little guided trail ride at a vacation spot—not places where horses are an integral part of the vacation experience, like on a "dude ranch," but those places on the side of the road or where a trail ride is part of a larger tourism site. These horses do several rides a day usually in group outings, where a dozen or so people in sneakers and shorts with cameras strapped around their necks climb into the saddle. There is a "bridle path" that the horses know by heart. There is usually a most-amicable order that the horses go in. The rider could basically drop the reins and let the horse follow the horse ahead of them. You would get a sense of the dullness of the horse if you were to try to take him off the trail (which most places request you don't do). The horse will almost immediately get bothered by being taken out of his comfort zone—his dull frame of mind. When he was in his routine mode, he could space out all those things that are a bit bothersome—Junior leaning off to one side, Mom jabbing at his mouth every time she snapped a picture. "Grin and bear it," he thinks, "I'll be back to the barn in thirty-seven minutes."

Taking that horse out of his routine is not fair to him and won't be fun for you. In fact, it could be dangerous if your mount decided that, if you aren't going to stick to the beaten path, he would beat the shortest path back to the security of the barn!

As a beginner, appreciate dullness. And when you become a more experienced equestrian, you will really appreciate how sensitive horses are.

The Mouth

The horse wears a leather bridle on his head that holds a metal bit in his mouth. Reins are attached to the bit on either side of the horse's face; those reins are held by the rider and are used to help control the horse.

Experienced riders have what are often referred to as "soft hands"; they are careful not to pull on the horse's mouth, and they use the bit as a communication tool in a very sensitive way. A horse that is ridden regularly by beginners typically has had his mouth pulled on a lot. Beginners often use the reins and the bit to help balance themselves in the saddle. This is another place where the lesson horse gets dull to some of the signals that a beginning rider is inadvertently giving him.

Tolerance

If you haven't figured it out by now, the horse that is used for lessons needs to have a very tolerant personality! When stables find good lesson horses, they don't let them go easily. Lesson horses work hard, sometimes giving several lessons a day, but they are also typically given excellent care—the smart lesson barn manager knows the value of the good lesson horse and the importance of keeping the horse healthy and on the payroll.

Choosing Your Lesson Horse

When you first begin to take lessons at a stable, the instructor will pick out a horse for you to ride; you probably won't be offered the choice between one horse or another. The instructor will assess your riding level and choose the horse from the string of lesson horses that is most appropriate for you.

Be patient. The matching process might take two or three lessons before you find the perfect horse for you to learn with. And be open to change. The instructor will suggest a different horse for you when the time is right, when you have exhibited the skills that you need to have to move up to a new, perhaps less "dull" horse.

Although you should expect that the instructor at a lesson barn will pick out the horse for you to ride in lessons, do speak up if for some reason you find the horse frightens you. For instance, perhaps you are short, and the horse picked for your lesson is very tall. If that intimidates you, no matter how perfect the horse is otherwise for your level of skill, you need to request a different horse and go back to the tall one when you are more confident.

Your Own Horse

Maybe you already own a horse or are in the process of acquiring one. Taking lessons even though you are already experienced is a wise and admirable thing to do. You might want to take lessons to learn a new discipline, perhaps you are concerned about some of the holes in your own or your horse's education, or maybe you just want to see how much better the two of you can get. Good idea!

Getting lessons on your own horse if you already board the horse at a boarding stable probably won't be difficult. Big boarding stables often have instructors available who can provide you with lessons.

Your barn might not have an instructor who can teach you the discipline you want to learn. You certainly don't have to move your horse just to get to a barn that does, although you might consider this down the road. You can choose to either truck your horse to an instructor's facility or you can get your instructor to come to you.

Truck-ins

The decision to truck your horse to another facility is limited by trailer availability. When you trailer your horse to a barn and take a lesson, you are referred to as a "truck in." This approach is great if you own a horse trailer or have a super kind friend who would lend you one once a week. You probably won't want to add trailering fees to your weekly lesson bill to have someone else truck your horse for you for a fee.

QUESTION?

What if I don't want to have my own horse? Can I just take lessons forever?

There's no reason you can't just keep on taking lessons for as long as you want. You do not have to own a horse to learn how to ride one. Owning your own horse is incredibly rewarding, but having a horse is also a huge commitment any way you look at it, so if you don't feel up to it, it's definitely best not to own a horse.

Instructor Visits

Having your instructor come to you is not uncommon. Many riding instructors do not have their own facility and rent space at one. Some might have clients come to them while others go to their clients. If you own a horse and want to bring an instructor to the barn where you keep him, you need to do a couple of things before you line this up:

- Make sure you find out from the barn manager or owner if it's okay for your instructor to come to the facility and give you a lesson on your own horse. There are liability issues here that need to be addressed; your barn will want to make sure they are covered for what you plan to do.
- Make sure the instructor has her own liability insurance that covers her on other people's property.

Your barn might request that you, your instructor, or probably both of you sign a liability release. Even though you probably signed one when you agreed to board there, this release will be specific to the lesson environment. If you don't feel comfortable signing it or your instructor won't sign it, you need to make other arrangements. It's perfectly acceptable for your barn to want to cover itself from all angles. A horse business is inherently fraught with potential lawsuits so releases are a must.

If you plan to have an instructor regularly give you lessons at your boarding barn, you will need to work around any other riders who are using the facility at the same time. People have limited time for their hobbies, and the other boarders cannot be expected to work around your lesson schedule. You and your instructor need to decide if this is okay. A lot depends on the size and activity level of the facility.

Lastly, if your instructor comes to your personal home/barn and gives you a lesson, you need to have an appropriate place to have the kind of lesson you want to have. If you want jumping lessons, but your barn has a tiny 40' × 50' riding ring with no jumps, this probably isn't going to work. Lessons are most productive in large arenas with some obstacles and other items the instructor could use to make the lesson interesting for everyone involved.

ALERT!

The phrase "bombproof" is often tossed around in the horse world to describe a horse that is a calm, steady mount—in other words, a good horse for a beginner to ride. However, you should be aware that there is not a horse on the planet that is totally bombproof—it might not be a bomb that sets him off, but every horse has some upper limit of what he can tolerate. Some horses have very specific distractions that bother them, but they might not encounter these often (snowmobiles, for instance) so it isn't too much of a problem.

Purchasing a Horse

Beginners who are thinking about buying a horse are smart to take lessons first. If you haven't picked out the perfect horse yet, lessons can help you decide what kind of horse you want. Are you comfortable on a horse of any height? Or do you need to look for horses that keep you somewhat close to the ground? Do you prefer a horse of a breed that carries his head and neck more parallel with the ground? Or do you like the feeling of the horse's head and neck more upright in front of you?

When you start looking for a horse to purchase, you are almost definitely going to want to ride him before you put your money down. Therefore, if you are new to riding or returning from a long hiatus, taking a few lessons before you begin your search will give you the confidence you need to ride potential purchases.

Which Breed?

Horse breeds have different kinds of gaits. All breeds (with a few exceptions) walk, trot, and canter. However, the trot of an Arabian has quite a lot of up-and-down movement (called "suspension" or "animation") and is quite a bit different from the trot of a Quarter Horse, which tends to have a more sturdy, shorter strided gait. Of course, individual animals all differ from each other, so you could find a Quarter Horse that bounces you around quite a bit at the trot.

It would be perfect if you could take lessons on the two or three different breeds of interest to you. Then you could have a real sense of the breed before you buy a horse of your own. Your instructor will be happy to give you some tips on whether the lesson horse you ride is typical of the breed.

FACT

Horses have athletic ability and tendencies just like humans. Some horses seem exceptionally well built for getting their huge bodies off the ground and over a jump; others have a build that makes them good at the sprinting and sharp turns needed to compete in games like barrel racing. Figure out what you want to do with a horse and then look for a suitable horse to do it with. Don't expect the sprinter to excel at doing cross country or foxhunting. Your horse will enjoy his job more if he is well suited to it, and will make riding more enjoyable for the rider.

Shopping with Help

Your instructor might be willing to help you find a horse. Some instructors actually do that as part of their business and might help you make arrangements to go see a horse. Others simply are willing to come along (for a fee to cover their time, of course) to look with you at horses you have found on your own. You might check ahead with your instructor to see if she is willing to test ride a prospective horse for you—after the owner or someone the owner designates rides the horse for you.

Vet Check

Before you bring a horse home, give the seller a deposit and arrange for a veterinarian of your choosing to examine the horse in what is called a "Pre-Purchase Exam" or "Vet Check." This exam will involve the basics—temperature, respiration, lameness exam, etc. Inform the veterinarian what you plan to do with the horse so that the horse can be checked appropriately. For instance, if you plan to jump the horse, it would probably pay to have its legs and feet checked out more thoroughly, even including X rays. If you plan to breed the horse, you might want to have a full reproductive exam done. Keep in mind that the vet check does not encompass a "pass" or "fail." It simply assesses the overall health of the horse, keeping in mind your plans.

ALERT!

Don't underestimate the value of the mixed breed horse. They tend to cost less since they are not registered and are, therefore, considered less "valuable." Some actually can be registered, such as Half-Arabs (Arabians are often crossed with many different breeds), National Show Horses (Arabian and Saddlebred crosses), and the associations that register horses based solely on color such as buckskin, palomino, or paint horses. But even if the horse isn't registered, unless you are planning to breed a mare or show in the breed association shows, mixed breeds can make the best riding horses.

Leasing a Horse

Leasing a horse can give you the best of all worlds if you go about it the right way. Leasing gives you a chance to enjoy the horse as if it were your own without the long-term commitment of purchasing a horse outright. There are a few different ways to lease a horse, and a few legal issues you need to consider.

Private Leases

It's very common in the horse world for a person to get a horse, enjoy it for a few years, then find that his or her life circumstances have changed and that he or she no longer has enough time for the horse. This is a common result for women who get pregnant and teenagers who go off to college. But it also occurs when people change jobs and need to commute long distances or do more business-related travel than when they first got the horse. Conscientious horse owners who find themselves in these circumstances will begin to search for someone to spend some time with the horse. Perhaps the horse owner can ride the horse on weekends but would like to find someone who can groom and ride the horse a couple of times during the week.

If you take lessons at a barn where horses are boarded, let the barn manager know you're interested in leasing a horse. There might be just such a circumstance at the barn. The barn manager might say, "You know, Susan used to come four or five times a week, but she got a new job, and we're lucky if we see her once on the weekends. Maybe she'd like someone to spend some time with Spirit. I'll ask and let you know." Look around in the same papers and bulletin boards where you would look if you were seeking to buy a horse. Tell everyone in your group of horse friends.

You will hear a couple of terms when it comes to leasing a horse from someone:

- **Free lease:** This means that the owner will essentially hand over the horse to you, and you can ride it anytime you like, no money will exchange hands. There will probably be some upfront discussion about what type of riding you can do with the horse (see the discussion about leasing agreements at the end of this section). But mostly you treat the horse as if it were your own, and you will be the only one riding it and paying all the expenses.

- **On-farm or in-barn lease:** In a lease arrangement like this, the requirement is that the horse remains where it is. This might be at the owner's home, or it might be at the boarding barn where the owner keeps it.

Leasing the Lesson Horse

Lesson barns often lease their lesson horses for use on the property. Typically they offer what is known as a "half-lease." You can usually find signs on the bulletin board at the barn listing horses that are available for partial lease. You pay a certain amount of money each month—usually half of the barn's typical monthly boarding fee—and you are allowed to ride two or three times per week. Typically, you pick specific days of the week that the horse is "yours" to ride. Some arrangements get even more specific— i.e., Tuesday afternoon, Thursday evening, and anytime Saturday. In these cases, the horse might also be used for lessons or is partial-leased by someone else too, or even both.

ESSENTIAL

You don't want the horse you lease to have colic. Colic is defined as simply a bellyache. But when you are talking about a half-ton animal with several hundred feet of complicated gastrointestinal tract, a bellyache is a huge deal. Colic is perhaps the most common reason that horses die. A horse will kick up at his stomach with a hind foot, bite at his sides, refuse food, not produce manure, stretch out as if trying to relieve himself, and roll violently when he is experiencing a colic episode. The most important action is calling the veterinarian immediately.

Some partial leases also include a lesson a week. Or they might include bringing the horse along with the rest of the barn group to a horse show or riding the horse in a show that takes place at the barn.

Partial-leasing of lesson horses allows the barn to keep a substantial string of horses with different skills and at different levels to use specifically for lessons. Between lessons and leasing, the horse pays for its keep and then some.

Beware of barns that seem to stretch their horses' energy too thin. The horse you lease should be in excellent health with plenty of flesh, not thin and bedraggled looking. Often, horses at boarding barns are kept in stalls too much, and these horses really need to get out and have some fresh air and exercise. The more often the horses are ridden, the more they look forward to going back to their stall, taking a nap, and being left alone!

The Lease Agreement

Like everything you do in life that involves risk and other people's property, you should expect to sign a "lease agreement." This legal document should spell out everything involved with leasing the horse including:

- What kind of food the horse should be fed.
- Where the horse is to be kept and/or under what kind of conditions it should be kept (i.e., a run-in shed is sufficient or a full box stall, what kind of fencing, etc.).
- Any financial information, such as who pays for medical attention, special supplements, shoeing, etc.
- What the exact procedure should be in a medical emergency and which of you will ultimately be responsible for the bill.
- What happens if the horse dies while under your care.

Of course you don't expect dire situations to happen, but it's certainly within the realm of possibility. Horses get hurt and, yes, they die. Sometimes suddenly. Your leasing agreement should cover all potential scenarios.

Before you agree on a private lease, have someone else look over the lease agreement. Of course, a lawyer is always important when it comes to legal documents, but you also want an experienced horse person to look it over as well.

Lastly, to lease a horse from anyone, you want to have some good references on hand. Riding instructors, veterinarians (even if it's your dog or cat vet), and personal references would all help you.

FACT

Some insurers focus specifically on equine insurance. If you decide to lease a horse, investigate liability insurance that covers situations in which the horse injures someone (biting and kicking), or in which the horse gets out of the pasture, gets hit by a car, and someone in the car is injured. Be sure to protect yourself.

Chapter 7

Horse and Riding Safety

Horses are inherently dangerous. They are large, heavy animals with a very strong sense of self-preservation. Their first defense from perceived danger is flight. Combine that with a relatively small human being who hasn't learned how to interact with horses, and it can be like throwing gasoline on glowing embers. But there are ways to be safe around horses.

Safety Basics

Even before you consider safety equipment in the barn and in riding, there are things you can do to ensure a safe environment for you and your horse. To increase the safety of being around horses:

- Create a safe environment around the barn.
- Teach your horse to be respectful.
- Learn how to handle horses safely.
- Teach your horse to move his feet in any direction at your request.
- Always seek to increase your horsemanship skills.
- Always learn from a teacher whose horsemanship you admire.

FACT

Watch a horse walk over rough or rocky ground, and notice that she will, even at a pretty good pace, avoid the rocks in the path with all four feet. A horse's keen awareness of where it's stepping (even though the feet are directly underneath her and mostly within a blind spot) is called "proprioceptiveness." (Humans and all animals, by the way, have this ability too.) Horses that are kept in dirt paddocks and ridden only in smooth dirt arenas lose a bit of this ability—which is why a lot of horses ridden almost exclusively in arena-focused disciplines can seem pretty clumsy out on the trails.

A Safe Barn Environment

Safety starts with the barn and the environment in which you ride and handle horses. With your own barn, you have complete control. Being very particular about the barn environment leads to a better safety record. When you ride horses at riding stables and other facilities, be sure to pick a stable that has good barn management with safety as a top priority. Here are some things to consider for your own stable or to assess when you are checking out a place to ride.

The Aisle

While there are many things to load up a horse barn with, keep clutter to a minimum. You want to be able to lead a horse in and out of a stall or corral to the area where you tack up without the potential of tripping over something. Everything should be in its place, i.e., neatly hung, stacked, or stored out of the way. The aisle of the barn should especially be kept free and clear at all times. You shouldn't have to spend an hour clearing out the aisle just to bring a horse in to saddle her.

Saddle racks and bridle holders in the aisle should be available where you can reach your tack easily while you are getting your horse ready to ride. These items shouldn't be in your way, and saddle racks should be of a type that would be safe around horses; for example, they shouldn't have sharp metal edges; and if they fold down, they should fold flat out of the way against the wall.

Tie rings should be up high enough (at least horse shoulder height) so a tied horse cannot get a leg over the rope. Tie your horse to a post or other thing that she can't pull out of the ground or out of the wall. Many a horse and human have been injured by a horse dragging an 8-foot post around that had been sunk only 2 or 3 feet into the ground. Yes, horses are that strong. And they are typically alarmed by a post following them around. So don't expect, if that happens, they are going to calmly stand there and wait for you to detach this sudden new appendage. Some will, but many won't.

It's not good to have smooth surfaces around a barn. Concrete aisles should be covered with rubber mats or should have a textured surface. Wash areas should have rubber matting with holes to drain water off and provide a safe standing area, especially when wet and covered with suds. Horses are pretty good with their feet, but it's still important to make sure that mats are flat and that there aren't booby traps that the horse could trip over.

The Paddocks

Gates should open easily and swing wide so your horse can't get caught between the gate and the fence post that it latches to, and especially so you aren't caught between that thousand-pound horse and the post. Not only should the gates swing wide, but you should be sure to actually swing them wide when you take a horse out of a corral (although you need to consider whether other horses might come out too!). Sliding doors are best for stalls; like swinging doors, slide them completely open when you take a horse out of a stall.

If you have to take a horse out of a paddock that holds several other horses, it's best to simply find someone to tend the gate for you to make sure no other horse slips out with yours. The information in the next few sections about respectful horses and your horse being able to move any foot in any direction at your request is the key to good horse behavior, but if you are riding other people's horses, those expectations can be unrealistic.

Fences should be in good repair and be horse safe. Inexpensive electric fencing is safe for horses, but be sure to consider two significant cautions. First, ensure that the horse is accustomed to electric fencing. Second, ensure that the fence posts (often metal or fiberglass) used to hang the electric strands (available in wire, rope, or tape) are either safely rounded on the top or are tall enough so that a horse could not jump on one and get impaled on the other (another common occurrence in the horse world). You want to spend your time riding not doctoring injuries.

E ALERT!

If you feel something is beginning to be uncomfortable when handling or riding your horse, seek help. Don't simply hope the situation will get better on its own, because often it won't. A situation as seemingly simple as a horse that is starting to get grouchy at feeding time can deteriorate into one that is quite serious. Choose your mentors wisely—and take their advice. Sometimes it takes just a couple of adjustments in your approach to make the situation better.

The Riding Arena

A riding arena should be reserved for just that—riding. Tractors, horse trailers, and other equipment should not be stored there unless they are cordoned off by horse-safe fencing. The fencing of the arena should be safe and solid—wood posts with wood rails are still the best option. This kind of fencing is highly visible to the horse and is probably going to be the least damaging if you fall off and land on it. Don't put up metal fence posts that you could be impaled on if you land on one. Vinyl fencing has become popular, but it can splinter and be quite sharp when broken (especially in cold climates).

The footing of an arena should be appropriate. Grass can be very slippery in the morning dew or after a rain when riding a horse with steel shoes. Some mix of sand and sawdust, gravel and stone dust, or many other combinations can be just perfect for horses. The footing should not be too thick, since horses could develop tendon problems from slogging through heavy sand day after day.

A Respectful Horse

The best way to be safe around horses is for the horses you interact with to be respectful of humans. This does not mean instilling fear in them. In fact, a fearful horse has a lot more potential of being dangerous than one that is simply uneducated.

Some things that indicate that a horse is respectful of humans are:

- He keeps a safe "bubble" of space around you—he can keep his distance and still be comfortable. A horse that is always chumming up right beside you will be on top of you if he spooks before you have a chance to react.
- He allows you to walk into his stall without crowding the door or turning his butt toward you. A horse that turns his butt to people when they enter the stall is probably feeling defensive. Figure out what that is causing it, and fix it.
- If you are cleaning manure out of a paddock with a horse in it, the horse doesn't breathe down your neck. He likes to be with you, and that's nice. But you are a lot smaller than he is, and he keeps a respectful distance away while still being "with" you.

- He leads well, moving off when he feels the slack begin to come out of the lead rope. You don't have to beg him to lead, he doesn't plant his feet or lead out in a big rush.
- He stands while being tacked up and while waiting for you to mount.

A horse that moves off the second you are in the saddle is probably feeling like you are giving him a signal to move off. Become aware of how you mount and sit and adjust your reins, etc. What are you doing with your legs? Your seat? Don't just grumble about this no-good so-and-so that won't stay still; horses are usually just doing what they think they are supposed to be doing.

Always get help from someone who is more experienced when it comes to handling disrespect in horses. A horse is rarely mean for no reason; instead he feels that he needs to defend himself. Whether it's logical in your eyes or not doesn't matter since it's logical to the horse. And it doesn't have to be "abuse" that caused the defensiveness. Some extremely sensitive horses are frightened by people who are rather gruff and a bit abrasive in their actions and voice. Horses are pretty good at picking up on someone's intent, but some extra sensitive horses take things harder than others.

If the person you turn to for help solves an issue like a horse turning his butt to you in the stall by getting out a dressage whip or by some other harsh method, find someone else to learn from. Punishing this way only makes a fearful horse more defensive and puts the handler in more danger.

Handling Horses

There are as many techniques for handling horses as there are people handling them. What you want to learn are the safe techniques. There are some general rules of thumb that will help you be safer when leading a horse.

First, never wrap a lead rope or longe line that is attached to a horse around your wrist or arm. If a horse spooks while you are leading him from one place to another or while you are simply standing holding him or letting him graze, you don't want to have the lead wrapped tightly around a body part. You could be dragged, have your arm pulled out of the socket, or even have a finger taken off.

Many people teach a horse to lead by holding it tight under the chin. This is very confining for the horse. A big animal needs some room to move. If you are afraid the horse is going to jump on you, you might need to consider whether the methods you (or others) are using are causing him not to be respectful. If a horse spooks while you are holding him right at the clip under his chin, where does he have to jump to except right on top of you? If you give him a foot or two of lead rope, he has a foot or two of jumping space without being on you.

When you approach a horse to catch him in the corral, hold your hand out a little in a friendly gesture. Give the horse a little rub, slip the lead around his neck, and halter him. A horse that has been well trained will help you slip the halter on by lowering his head and turning to place his nose in the halter noseband. Again, when you are handling lesson horses, you might find that the inconsistency with which these horses are handled often doesn't allow for this kind of smooth interaction. But it's an admirable goal with any horse you handle.

Be aware of the environment while you lead the horse to the barn. Are there obstacles to consider? Are there pieces of equipment in the way now? Is the horseshoer in the aisle at one end working on a horse? If so, take the other entrance. If you are coming up on a blind doorway, let people know you are coming.

These are just a few of the things you should consider while handling the horse. This topic could fill an entire book all on its own. The key is to constantly be aware of your environment and of the horse.

FACT

Research has shown that horseback riding contributes greatly to traumatic head injury (TMI) statistics. Reports show that adults ages twenty-five or older account for at least 54 percent of hospital-treated rider injuries; head injuries are associated with more than 60 percent of equestrian-related deaths; and wearing ASTM-certified helmets lower these statistics. The math is simple.

Directing the Horse's Feet

Your riding instructors might teach you things like "emergency dismounts" or heading a runaway horse toward a wall in the arena. Both of these actions might certainly get the job done and perhaps are appropriate in a real emergency where you can't think of anything else. However, there is a lot better way to get a runaway horse to stop or to get yourself back to a safer situation so that you don't have to jump off. The alternative method, however, includes a lot of preparation and time up front on the part of whoever trains the horses you ride. And this method requires follow up and understanding on your part.

If this book could have only one topic, it would be the importance of a horse knowing how to move each of his feet in any direction at your request. This is most critical for safely, effectively, and pleasurably riding horses. There are a couple of other topics that come into play, but when you can direct the movement of a horse's feet—either from the saddle or on the ground—you are about as safe as you are ever going to be when involved with horses.

FACT

A good rule of thumb around a barn is to always latch gates behind you no matter what. This way, it just becomes a habit. Horses are remarkable at detecting a gate that's not secure—some will constantly test the gate by pushing it with their noses. Loose horses could cause danger to other people, to vehicles on the road, or to other riders. They could injure themselves when getting into spaces that are not designed for them or onto floors that are not secure enough for their weight. The horse could also get into grain or eat too much rich grass or flowers and ornamental plants that are poisonous to horses.

The Runaway

A horse "runs away" with his rider because he is afraid of something. The experienced rider knows how to shut down the runaway pretty fast. This kind of rider sits up straight and deep in the saddle to instill some confidence in the horse, showing support for the horse when situations that might make him fearful arise. Fearful riders usually bend forward instead of sitting up straight when a horse makes a sudden move. This kind of rider often grips with his knees and feet in an effort to stay on, but this only frightens the horse more and often causes a worse situation.

Most horses you will ride for lessons have been taught if they "spook" (jump at something that startles them), they can jump without bolting off into the sunset. Other horses, and certain horses with particular fears, will simply need to jump and then run.

Horses get their forward impulsion from the hindquarters—that's where their engine is. If a horse is running away, it seems logical that slowing the engine down will slow the horse down. You can teach a horse that when you pull up on one rein to bend his head and neck toward you, and perhaps add putting your leg on that same side against his belly or flank area, he should step his hind leg sideways on that side. Even a little sideways motion will slow the horse's forward movement. The deeper you get the horse stepping under his belly, the more he shuts down his impulse to run, and the faster you can get him stopped. In Chapter 9 on "The Trot" you will learn that a barely perceptible movement similar to this is called a "half halt."

Most stables have crossties in the aisle. Basically, these are lead ropes attached to each side of the aisle wall to clip both leads from the horse's halter to. Be sure your horse is accustomed to crossties before you use them. Crossties can be extremely dangerous if a horse gets spooked, runs forward, comes to the end of the two crossties, and flips over backward. Be sure any crossties have "quick release" safety snaps on the ends attached to the wall.

Getting One Horse Out of a Corral of Horses

Another place you will find directing the feet to come in handy is when you are trying to get a horse out of a corral when his corral mates would like to come along. With a horse that has learned to move his feet at the rider's direction, you can open the gate as wide as necessary without being wide enough for other horses to come through. Then you can ask the horse to step through the gateway. When he clears the gate, ask him to step his hindquarters around so he is facing you, so you never have to let go of the gate. A respectful horse will then stand patiently while you latch the gate.

Trailer Loading

Without being able to direct the horse's feet, how would you load him in a trailer? Horses will often step off to the side of the trailer to try to avoid going on. Most people will walk the horse back away from the trailer several feet, turn him around, and start again. By walking the horse away from the trailer, you have rewarded him for evading the trailer. If you can direct the horse's feet, you never have to change your position to load him on the trailer. First, direct his feet to have him looking in the trailer. Next, when he is paying attention to the inside of the trailer, reward him by allowing him time to think about it. When he moves off or moves his attention from the trailer, bring his attention back. A horses is curious and wants to do the right thing—but the right thing has to be clear to him. Finally, by being able to direct his feet while standing a few feet away at the other end of the lead rope, you will easily help him figure out trailers. And jumps. And water crossings. And bridges. The list of ways you can help your horse is endless.

From the Saddle

Novice riders think of the reins being attached to the bit which is, of course, in the horse's mouth. In reality, this is true. But theoretically, the reins are attached to the horse's feet. When the horse's feet are moving, and you pick up on a rein, you want a foot to move. When the horse is moving forward, you should be able to pick up on the left rein, and, if the horse is just about to lift up his left foot, draw the rein out to the left. The horse will move his foot out of his straight path of travel and out to the left. When you pick up on that rein and draw it toward you enough to bend his head a little, you should be able to get the left hind foot to step under his belly slightly. This is how you can direct the horse's feet from the saddle.

Why is this helpful? If you can direct his feet accurately from the saddle, you can get through gates without getting off your horse, you can get him up to a mounting block to dismount (or, even better, mount), you can avoid obstacles on the trail, you can direct him toward a jump. Almost everything you want to do on a horse besides be simply a passenger, you can do with finesse and accuracy by teaching a horse to move his feet at your direction.

Increase Your Skill

Even the most accomplished horsemen and horsewomen will admit they feel they still have much to learn. Horses are complex creatures and riding them can be a lifelong challenge. Experience and working with many different horses can increase your skill exponentially. Another important way to increase your horsemanship is to ride and be around horses on a regular basis.

The horse knows everything you think you need to teach him before a human ever comes near: backing up, cantering on different leads, trotting, putting his head down. These are not actions you need to teach him. But you hope to teach him to do all these actions when you ask him. To learn how to teach a horse to do your bidding takes a lot of hard work. It's not the horse that is the key learner in this partnership, it's the person.

To work with horses, you have an obligation to learn to interact with a horse in a way that is fitting to him. The horse is the captive one—he did not ask to be a pet, to be ridden, or locked in a stall or corral. In captivity, the horse does not pick the herd in which he is most comfortable and most welcome, he has to make do with the herd he is put into.

Equestrians owe it to the horses they ride to constantly increase their skill level. Even instructors have teachers. If you always seek to increase your skill, most horses you come in contact with will try to meet you part way.

Learning from Mentors

It takes a village to teach someone good horsemanship. You will encounter lots of horsemen and horsewomen in your equestrian pursuits. Most people in the horse industry are sincere, horse-loving, kind, well-intentioned people. But just because someone is kind doesn't mean you have to take lessons from her.

There is not just one way to interact with horses: people use conditioned response training, so-called "natural horsemanship," clicker training, and, sadly, physical abuse, and many other approaches, some of which are a mixture of several types. As you become more involved with horses, you will begin to lean toward a certain approach with your own horsemanship. Find people who mesh with that direction and stick with them.

If these methods aren't working, by all means, try something else! Horses, like people, all have different learning styles and different levels of intelligence and interest. Usually, however, a horse that isn't learning what we are trying to teach him needs us to refine our teaching methods.

Turn to your mentors when you're having a specific problem with your horse. If the people whose horsemanship you really admire also train young horses or teach lessons (assuming you are already taking lessons from her or him, which you should be), spend as much time with them as you can. Ask if you can watch some training sessions or some lessons. See what you can pick up that you can use to improve your own horsemanship or your specific situation.

And when you've become fairly proficient, be open to other people turning to you as a mentor. It's a good way to pay forward your mentors' help. Don't force yourself on people, however; just make it obvious that the invitation is there and let the person come to you.

Safety While Riding

The horse and the match between his level of training and your level of riding is perhaps one of the most important safety issues to consider when mounted. However, there are many other things to keep in mind.

Helmets—Again

It can't be emphasized enough: Always ride with a helmet. Helmets are a pain. They are a tad uncomfortable, a tad unattractive; and they are just awkward, and one more piece of equipment to remember. But after you have a situation where you could have made out better with a helmet, you would pay anything to turn the clock back ten minutes. With perhaps the exception of a spinal injury or cracking your skull, almost any injury you can sustain when falling off a horse is repairable. Even when all your friends are riding in baseball caps and cowboy hats, be sure to put on your helmet.

Tacking Up

One of the simplest safety precautions when tacking up a horse is to be sure all tack is in good condition. Anything that looks like it might break will—at the most inopportune moment. The next important thing is to be sure to buckle every buckle and do up every strap. Having a bridle strip off a horse's head when you are galloping down the trail is a little disconcerting, to say the least.

If the horse you ride has been taught respect for humans, you don't have to worry about being stepped on by a horse that won't stand still while being saddled. And if he has been carefully trained and properly handled, he will accept the saddle without tail wringing and prancing around.

You don't have to be on a horse's back drilling it in a particular maneuver for "training" to be taking place. Every time a human interacts with a horse, the horse is being trained. Walking into a corral or stall with a horse and feeding it sets up numerous opportunities to train him to behave well. You can set up good behaviors—such as standing politely back from the stall door with his head to you and waiting patiently for you to dump the grain into his bucket. Or you can set up negative and potentially dangerous behaviors like lunging at the bucket of grain in your hand before you've barely gotten the stall door open.

Mounting and Dismounting

Use a mounting block if you are not flexible enough or tall enough to comfortably mount your horse from the ground. You don't want to be halfway recumbent with one foot in the stirrup, bouncing up and down, trying to climb aboard when your horse decides to bolt because the gardener starts up the lawnmower. There is no shame in using conveniences when you can.

Don't mount, dismount, or ride in barn aisles or other confined spaces. Mounting and dismounting can be potentially the most dangerous times during your ride. Be cautious and be aware.

When you mount or dismount, which it's customary to do from the left (although it wouldn't hurt to teach your horse and yourself to be comfortable mounting and dismounting from the right), always have your left rein with enough contact to be able to quickly try to change your horse's mind if he decides to walk off while you are getting on or off. If your horse is inclined to drift off when you are getting on or off, don't accept that behavior. He can learn to stand still while you are getting on. If he moves before you are ready, set him back to the place where you started and let him wait until you ask him to move. Even the most fidgety horse can learn that this is the appropriate way to act.

Good horsemanship involves a lot of common sense. Be cautious, but not too cautious. Sometimes with horses, it's best to just get out and do what you want to do. If you always work to increase your awareness and consider the horse's perspective, you will be many steps toward good and safe relationships with horses.

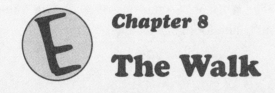

Chapter 8

The Walk

The horse's walk is, for horseback riding purposes, perhaps the most important gait of all. However, the walk might not be the gait you ride in most often, for example, for distance trail riding, you will trot a lot; for any kind of jumping, you will canter a lot. But the walk is the gait every other movement will start with. And it can be the most difficult gait to encourage the horse to move out in.

What Is the Walk?

The walk is the horse's slowest gait. The gait is determined by the number of footfalls in a complete "revolution" of all four feet. The number of footfalls in a walk is four—each of the four feet move off the ground separately. In the walk, when one foot is off the ground, the other three are touching the ground. Each footfall is called a "beat." So the horse's walk is a four-beat gait. Here's the order in which each foot falls:

1. Front foot
2. Opposite hind foot
3. Other hind foot
4. Other front foot

▲ Three of the horse's feet are touching the ground at a time while he walks.

FACT

The movement of an animal's feet is known as a "gait." There are slower and faster gaits. With the horse, the walk is the slowest gait, the gallop is the fastest, and the trot and the canter fall in between the walk and the gallop. The trot has many different variations that are called different names.

Observing the Walk

Watching horses move around when they are on their own is a great way to learn about their movement. When they are in the corral or pasture, they are moving more naturally than when a rider climbs on top of them; the rider not only shifts the horse's balance but also interferes with the horse's movement by trying to direct it. Spend as much time as you can simply observing horses. As you watch, try to imagine being on top of one of the horses and feeling the movement that you see.

Watch how the hip lifts upward when the horse puts his weight on a hind foot and lowers when the horse begins to bring the weight off the hind leg and extends it to move forward. Observe how the shoulder blade moves when the front leg moves. And don't forget the horse's head—that heavy appendage sticking way out in front of the bulk of the horse's body moves with every step the horse takes.

Becoming aware of these movements on the ground will make it easier to detect them when you are in the saddle. And these movements will show you when the horse is just about to lift his weight off a certain leg—which is exactly the moment that it's best to direct the movement of that leg.

When we get to the trot in Chapter 9, you will also see how observing, then feeling, the movement will help you choose the proper "diagonal" to begin to post with.

ALERT!

Just because the walk is slow and easy, don't think you can just sit up on the horse and read a book while he is walking. Given the right impetus—a noise in the bushes, a plastic bag flying by—any horse can go from a walk to a gallop in a couple of seconds. You certainly can let the reins loose and relax at the walk, but always be prepared to collect the reins and use your body to help calm and direct the horse if he moves quickly.

But before you can ride the walk, you have to catch, groom, tack up, and mount your horse.

Catching the Horse

Many lesson barns might have your horse already caught, groomed, and saddled for you so you can get right on and ride in the lesson when you arrive. However, if you want to learn more about horses in general, you'll want to learn to do these tasks yourself. In fact, you'll want to find an instructor who expects you to learn how to do these things.

If you are to tack your horse up yourself (and if you own your horse, you will be expected to!), your horse will probably be in a stall when you arrive for your lesson. If it's your first time riding a particular horse, ask the barn staff about his stall manners. You will want to know about a horse that tends to whirl and turn his hindquarters to you when you open the stall door! A good lesson barn will not let a novice deal with this kind of horse anyway; they will either have you ride a different horse or have this horse out of the stall and on crossties for you already.

Most horses, however, are very well mannered when a person enters his stall. Here are a few basics:

- Have the horse's halter hanging from your arm in a way that is organized for how you will put it on him. Have the lead rope attached and looped over your arm (but NOT wrapped around your arm in any way).
- If the horse is standing with his hindquarters to the stall door when you approach the stall, talk to him; most horses will turn to see who it is.
- After you determine that the horse is going to be mannerly with you, close the door behind you after you enter the stall.
- Give the horse a friendly rub and some kind words to let him be assured that you are someone he might want to spend some time with.
- Approach the horse from his left side, which is the side most horses are handled from, and put his halter on.
- Before you open the stall door, check to see if any other horse or person is coming down the aisleway; if the coast is clear, open the door the entire way and walk out first, leading your horse behind you.

Photograph by Bud McGrath

▲ A nice lovely walk along a sandy stretch of beach can be horse lover's heaven.

Photograph by Gena McGrath

▲ This young man is dong a nice job of calmly asking his horse to back up.

Sometimes you might have to catch a horse out in a paddock. Horses can be amazingly hard to catch in even the smallest pen if they associate people with something they don't want to do (like ride around in circles in an arena being bounced on by a novice rider). Although you will want to teach your own horses to be easily caught in any situation (another involved topic to be found in a training book), sometimes it can be more efficient and less traumatic for all involved to simply bring some grain or a treat with you. If at all possible, do not feed the treat by hand; after you've got a halter and lead rope on the horse, drop the treat in a feed bucket or even on the ground. Better yet, just bring the treat or grain in a bucket in the first place.

The food-bribing approach to catching a horse can be complicated if more than one horse is in the paddock where yours is. In this instance, you might want to catch your horse and give him the treat outside the pen. He will come to associate you with getting a treat and probably will become easy to catch.

Treats for horses are a complicated topic. It's best to improve your horsemanship to a level where treats are completely unnecessary. Sometimes, however, with horses in busy environments like riding stables, it's important to keep things as easy as possible. So if you give treats while getting respect from a horse, use them to your advantage. Horses that are disrespectful of humans will just be worse when food is part of the equation so using food to catch a disrespectful horse is not a solution. If it's your own horse, find someone to help you with the respect issue and to help you learn to catch a horse. If the horse belongs to the riding stable, you can't force the stable to teach their horses anything. Respect is a difficult thing to teach a horse that is handled by people of many levels of skill, so simply expect the stable to have such a horse caught for you before you arrive for your lesson.

ALERT!

A good lesson barn that is concerned with safety will not have students going out to pens holding multiple horses to catch their horse. If you are asked to do this, be sure someone teaches you how to take one horse out of a paddock while others are there. While it's something you want to learn to increase your skills handling horses, it can be dangerous until you learn some reliable techniques.

Grooming the Horse

Grooming a horse before riding is important for many reasons:

- For the horse's comfort, it's good to remove dirt from where you're going to place the saddle and bridle.
- You can clean packed dirt out of his feet, which can help avoid hoof diseases such as "thrush," a common bacteria disease that smells bad and makes a horse's feet hurt. You can remove small stones in the packed dirt that might bruise the horse's feet and cause lameness. And you want your horse to be as comfortable as possible when you are riding him.

- A good grooming is a good time to examine the horse's entire body, checking for scrapes and splinters or coat and skin problems.
- Grooming a horse is a great time to further develop your relationship with a particular horse, whether he is your own or the one you happen to be riding that day.

What tool you use to start your grooming depends on how much dried mud the horse has caked on him. If the horse you ride is allowed to live a natural life, he will probably roll in the dirt every day. If it has rained, he will happily roll in mud. This helps keep flies away, and it simply feels good— rolling is the horse's way of scratching himself all over, including the places he can't normally reach while standing.

If he's caked with dried mud, start with a rubber mitt or stiff brush. Start at the neck and brush from front to back, top to bottom, brushing the dried mud away from the horse and away from you. (If the mud is wet and the temperatures are favorable, he should probably simply be hosed down. You don't want to brush wet mud into the horse's coat.) Stiff brushes or metal combs intended to help shed a winter coat are okay to use on the horse's body but do not use these kinds of tools on the head or the legs of the horse.

Next, use a less stiff brush to brush away all the dried mud you've kicked up. This is the brush you can also use on the legs, especially if there is mud on the legs, which there probably is. Finally, use either a very soft brush or a towel to put a nice shine on the horse's mud-free coat. You can use this brush on the horse's face, although it's nice to keep a separate soft brush that is reserved especially for the face so you aren't brushing dried mud into the horse's eyes and nose. The towel can also be used to carefully wipe around his eyes and the outer, visible portion of the ears (known as the "pinna").

Pick out the horse's feet with a tool known as a hoof pick. There is a V-shaped soft pad at the back on the bottom of the horse's foot called the "frog." The frog has a channel on either side of it; scrap the mud out of this channel. Dig firmly—this is like cleaning under your fingernails—but not extremely hard. Usually any surrounding dirt will come out with the dirt in the channels beside the frog.

Lastly, brush the horse's mane, tail, and foretop. There are combs with moveable tines that are designed to brush these without pulling out too many hairs. Detangling products work great on manes and tails, but they can make your hands very slippery; they can leave a mane so slippery that you couldn't use it for an emergency handhold if you need it while riding. And whatever you do, don't get the detangling product on the horse where the saddle goes, it will never stay in place! These kinds of products are best left for when you aren't about to ride or when you are grooming for a show the next day.

Saddling the Horse

Have your saddle, saddle pad, bridle, and helmet ready and waiting at the place where you will be saddling your horse. Bring him out of his stall and lead him there—probably to a set of crossties in the barn aisleway.

We covered the actual saddling steps in Chapter 3. Never strap your helmet to the saddle unless you know the horse is okay with that—the slapping of the helmet against the saddle can make some horses jump or try to bolt; when they move fast, the helmet slaps even harder. Then they get even more wound up; it's a cycle worth avoiding. Simply strap the helmet on your own head; that way you won't leave it back at the barn or simply forget to do it up when you mount.

Mounting

Most stables have several mounting blocks scattered around. They might be objects made specifically for mounting horses or they might be other objects pulled into service as mounting blocks such as cement blocks or milk crates. Anything will do. If you think you will have a hard time getting up on the horse, do not even consider doing it without a mounting block. It's too hard on your body, too hard on the horse's body, and can put you in quite dangerous positions.

Like taking off and landing in the airline industry, mounting and dismounting can be the most dangerous parts of riding horses. You're not quite on, you're not quite off, and something spooks your horse—and typically you are off no matter which way you are headed. And unlike being bucked off or falling off when you are riding, being dumped in the process of mounting or dismounting can place you very close to the horse's feet.

Get your horse over to the mounting block—if you can't direct his feet well enough to get him close to it, then choose a mounting block you can move to where the horse is happy to stand still. Take any slack out of the reins, but don't pull them so tight you cause the horse to move backward. Put your left foot into the left stirrup. Place your left hand on the base of the horse's neck area and position your right arm over the back of the saddle and hold the right side of the back of the saddle with your right hand. Bounce a couple of times on your right leg and then bounce yourself into the saddle. Don't pull on the saddle with the right hand that's around the back—try to feel the right amount of pull to get yourself up there without pulling the saddle off to the left. Gently lower yourself into the saddle. As you do, head your right foot for the stirrup. (If you are riding in a Western saddle, the stirrups will always be hanging. If you are riding in an English saddle, remember to pull both stirrups down to the ends of the leathers before you mount).

ALERT!

When leading a horse with an English saddle on his back, always run the stirrups up the leathers. Tuck the leathers in through the stirrup holes to keep them from slipping down and to prevent them rubbing on the leather of the saddle itself and making a mark.

Voilà! You are on. Don't allow your horse to walk off the second your fanny hits the saddle. He should learn that he needs to wait for you to be ready and not go until he is asked to go. If your horse has not been taught this—just another touch of respect for the human/horse relationship—it's not difficult to teach him yourself. Sit deep and heavy in the saddle once you are on—this should be an indication to an educated horse that you are not riding, you are simply sitting. If this doesn't work, pull back on the reins and ask him to stop. (Some horses have been taught "voice commands" so you might be able to also ask him to "whoa" at the same time you pull back on the reins. If he knows voice commands well, "whoa" is all you need.) Keep doing this until he stops and waits for you to organize yourself—your feet are in the stirrups in a good position, your reins are gathered evenly, etc.

Walking "In Hand"

The act of leading a horse with a halter and lead rope is referred to as "in hand," especially in the show ring. Outside the show ring, it's simply called "leading" your horse.

You want your horse to lead at a walk with a loose bit of lead rope dangling from his halter to your hand. Let the horse lead at or just behind your shoulder. And request that he walk a few steps away from you, a respectful distance so that if he spooks at something he is not immediately on top of you! Horses are not puppies—if they step on you even by accident, you could quickly have a broken foot. And besides the physical pain and the financial pain of the hospital bill, any devoted rider knows that an injury means lost riding time!

If your horse wants to walk right on top of you, doing something like swinging your arms around until they bump into him or otherwise letting the horse begin to think that perhaps he should stay a few feet away from this especially clumsy human is a good way to get the horse to think it was his own idea to stay a few feet away. A horse seems to be more relaxed about our requests if he believes it's his own idea.

And when you are leading a horse at a walk, he should be walking. If the horse is trotting beside you and you don't want him to be trotting, try slowing your pace down a little. Perhaps you are simply walking too fast for him! If he is trotting because he is all wound up about something, you are going to need to find a way to let him move his feet and get some energy out before you will be able to successfully lead him at a walk. If he is *always* this way, then he probably needs to get a lot more exercise than he is getting. What is enough exercise for one horse might be nowhere near enough for another.

If the horse is usually quiet to lead, there could be any number of things getting him a little wound up today. Perhaps the wind is blowing a bit hard, perhaps the temperatures have cooled down, and he is feeling pretty good, perhaps he is frustrated that he has to leave his friends. How you deal with each of these situations could be different (and different for different horses) and is best left to a book on training horses. However, one generality can be made: You need to remain calm and walk slowly to encourage your horse to follow your lead. If you get wound up and yell at him and swing the lead rope around wildly, you will not help your cause. Horses are naturally inclined to be influenced by other herd members, including you. If you have ever watched a group of horses grazing in a field or eating from the hay pile in a paddock, you'll see that if one horse lifts his head to gaze at the horizon where a person is walking toward the barn, all the horses will lift their heads and look in that direction. If one horse decides to flee toward a perceived safer area, all the horses will flee. You need to be the calming factor.

FACT

Horses can scare people—some people more than others. If you are new to horses or still a novice, you want to be handling horses only under supervision. Then if the horse scares you for whatever reason, you have someone to help. Under no circumstances should you be made to feel silly because you are afraid. You have a right to your emotions, and fear is an emotion. And rest assured, if you are among good teachers, the more you handle and ride horses, the less afraid you will become.

Riding the Walk

Riding the walk is mostly a piece of cake. You want to encourage a nice, lively walk. Both you and your horse should feel and act like you are really going somewhere, not dragging along like you are both sorry you ever met. While some horses have naturally livelier walks than others, all horses can move out well at the walk. If you think they can't, just watch them when they are out on their own! Or wait until you are turned around on the trail and heading back to the barn! If you can keep them in the walk at all, it will definitely be a lively walk.

That is the walk you want to strive for at all times—the one the horse picks up on his own when you are headed to the barn. To get the horse to walk out like this, you might need your body to be quite clear that this is what you want. If you sit stiff and inflexible, your horse will feel that in his back and move stiffly and inflexibly. Move your hips back and forth with the horse's hip movements. Liven and lighten up your seat. And when the horse moves out, move with him.

Some Walk Exercises

There are some fun little exercises you can do to learn to enjoy the horse at the walk and to help your horse understand about moving out. These are the kinds of exercises you can do to learn how to be particular about what you ask of your horse. If you learn to be particular from the beginning, your horsemanship level will move forward in leaps and bounds. If you "yahoo" around for a while, you will be at the disadvantage of trying to fix bad habits. But that can be interesting, too!

Exercises are great learning tools for both you and your horse. But don't drill your horse (and yourself) to boredom. Try an exercise a few times, then move on to something else. Go back to the exercise again during your ride, or the next time you ride. But don't repeat and repeat and repeat. Quit on a good note, and go ride off down the trail.

Close Your Eyes

Find an experienced horseperson who can walk your horse at the end of a leadrope. Mount up, have her walk your horse around, and while the horse is walking, close your eyes. Sometimes it's easier to feel the movements the horse makes by closing out visual distractions. Don't do this on your own! With someone reliable to walk your horse, you can concentrate on how the horse feels and not worry about what the horse is doing.

Up and Down

Add to the experience in the previous exercise by feeling for the movement of a particular leg. Pick out, say, the right hind leg and have your handler tell you every time the horse lifts that leg off the ground—now, now, now. When she says "now," pay attention to what you are feeling. The hind leg is a good one for this eyes-closed exercise because the large hip bone has a lot of movement to feel. Once you've done that a bit, take it one step further— you tell your handler when the right hind leg is lifting off the ground.

Learning these movements can help you be more than just a passenger on your horse—you can really learn how to work with the horse's movement to do exactly what you want to do.

Alternate Between Fast and Slow

Wherever you are riding—in an arena, out in the barnyard, or out on the trail—pick a spot 100 or so feet away and walk toward it. See how fast you and your horse can walk toward it. Then see how slowly you can walk toward the next object. Look up and ahead to your target. See what ways you need to alter your body position to get the rate of speed you desire. Can you get your horse to walk slowly without picking up on the reins but just by making yourself heavier in the saddle and not "riding" the horse so energetically? What does it take to get your horse to really walk out? More energy from you in the saddle? Bumping your legs against his sides? A bit of encouragement on the rump with the end of one of the reins or a crop?

Remember, you are always aiming for doing as little as possible. Always start out with the way you would *like* to ask your horse to do what you want. Then do what it takes to get there.

Alternate between slow, fast, and in between. Be consistent in how you ask for each and what your body is telling your horse at each pace. Alternating speeds gives the horse some points of comparison to learn and remember: "Ah, when she feels like that, I am supposed to walk this fast."

ALERT!

Do not hand feed horses under any circumstances, especially if they are not your own. Getting food this way is not a natural circumstance that horses find in nature. Although many people would dispute this, nature would show that horses do not seem to relate food to affection. Horses can quickly get nippy looking for treats.

Chapter 9
The Trot

The horse's trot is perhaps its most useful gait. Horses with a good trot can cover lots of ground with the least amount of effort. This is a gait that lesson riders will work in often. And dressage riders will need to perform several different levels of the trot.

What Is the Trot?

The trot is a two-beat gait. In the trot, the diagonal pairs of legs move at the same time: the front right and rear left leg move forward at the same time; the front left and rear right move forward at the same time. If you listen to a horse travel at the trot on a hard surface, you will hear the two beats.

FACT

There are other types of two-beat gaits that some breeds of horses do instead of the classic trot. The "pace" is familiar to anyone who has watched Standardbred racehorses (the horse that pulls the rider on cart called a sulky). The pace is a two-beat gait like the trot, except that the two legs on the same side of the horse land at the same time. It's an unusual gait to ride, but it's a fast gait at the races!

As with anything to do with horseback riding, it's helpful to observe horses moving on their own. Watch a loose horse and observe the movement of his shoulders and the movement of his hips while he trots. The shoulder moves forward as the front leg moves forward, the hip rises with the hind leg.

These are the movements you need to learn to ride with. If you post, you need to feel the hip thrust your hips forward to indicate when to start rising on the correct right diagonal. If you sit the trot, you will need to feel these movements to absorb them into your legs, ankles, and lower back.

▲ The horse moves diagonal pairs of legs at the same time when he trots.

Besides watching the loose horse trot out, also watch how a trotting horse slows down to the walk when he is trotting. Or how he downshifts from the trot to the stop. It's important to know how to work within this movement so you can slow down with him instead of slamming into his back at the downward transition.

Learning to Ride the Trot

It's helpful to learn to ride the trot on a horse that has a trot that doesn't have a lot of "action." While it's difficult to generalize on anything to do with horses, some breeds are likely to have a less animated trot than others. However, the trot depends on the education of the horse. A horse with a more advanced education learns to collect himself better and round his back under the rider, making the trot easier for the rider to get in rhythm with.

Western saddles have a couple of significantly different styles. One, known as the "swell fork," has humps on either side of the horn. The other style slopes off the sides of the horn and is known as a "slick fork." The slick-fork Western saddle is a bit easier to post in than the swell fork.

If you are just learning to ride, you will want to have a good working walk down first (see Chapter 8) before you move up to the trot. Everything is exaggerated at a faster gait, both good and bad, so if you feel you are out of sync with the horse at the walk, you will be way out of sync at the trot, and at the canter you would probably be doing little more than trying to stay on!

Spend some time at that good working walk. Here are three things to check before you move your horse up to the trot:

1. Is your lower torso, especially your hips, moving with the rhythm of the horse?
2. Is your upper body still but not rigid?

3. Are your arms and legs still? You need to be sure that you are not bumping with your feet when the horse is already going (remember that part a while back on how to make your horse dull?) and that you are not bumping on his mouth with your reins and the bit.

If you feel pretty good about those three things while you are moving at a nice fast walk, then it's time to move you and your horse up to the trot!

ALERT!

Refining your horse's transitions from one gait to the other will create a smooth-going horse. You should also aim to learn to make your own transitions smooth so that you aren't banging on your horse's back when he goes from a faster gait to a slower one. Likewise, when going from a slower gait to a faster one (called "upward transitions"), you should learn to get your body in the rhythm and position that the new gait requires.

When you are first asking your horse for a new move, don't get impatient. Reward your horse with verbal praise, a rub on the neck, or just a nice release of the aids to encourage him. Don't immediately ask for more. If he takes a few haunches-in steps, settle for that, and build on it the next time. A horse appreciates knowing he's done a good job, and he will give a little more each time.

As they say, Rome wasn't built in a day. A refined horse and a good rider weren't created in one session either. And the horse seems to develop exponentially. A few strides leads to several strides that quickly leads into a complete revolution of the ring, which before long becomes an immediate response every time you ask.

Posting

Posting—also known as "rising"—is the action of rising out of the saddle and returning to the saddle with each movement of the trot.

Photograph by Bob Atkins

▲ The rider rises as the horse's outside front leg moves forward.

Rising to the trot means posting on the proper diagonal pair of legs, known simply as the "diagonal." When the front leg of the horse that is next to the rail (or the wall of the indoor arena) moves forward, the rider rises out of the saddle. When the leg moves back, the rider sits. When you are first learning to post to the trot, you will want to look down at the horse's shoulder to see whether you are rising on the correct diagonal. Your goal is to learn to feel which leg is rising so you can rise without looking down.

You don't need to rise high out of the saddle. The point is simply to move more smoothly with the trot instead of bouncing. How high you rise can depend on how fast your horse trots. You will rise longer and higher on a horse with a long lazy trot (or you need to kick him up into a real working trot!) than you would with a horse with a short quick trot motion.

The rising trot is typically thought of as an English riding technique. But Western-style riders post as well. While you will not see posting by Western riders in the Western pleasure show ring, you certainly will see working Western riders rise to the trot during work sessions and out on the trail. The point of posting is to ride the horse's trot more smoothly—the horse doesn't care which saddle is on his back.

So don't be afraid to post in a Western saddle. Depending on the style of the saddle (see the sidebar on "slick forks" versus "swell forks"), a Western saddle might be more confining when it comes to rising at the trot so you will need to consider that.

The Sitting Trot

Once you get the hang of posting, you might wonder why anyone sits the trot anyway! However, if you plan to ride in Western classes at shows, you will need to sit the Western jog. This is typically not too hard since the very nature of the "jog" is a nice slow trot—in fact, over the last decade or so the jog has become so slow you almost can't tell the horse is in the trot gait. Even your ninety-year-old great grandmother could sit the Western jog.

In English classes, you will post at the trot most of the time. But some classes require the sitting trot, and sometimes judges will use it in classes when the winner is a toss up. In the dressage arena, you will definitely be required to sit the trot during part of the test, at least beyond the beginner levels.

To sit the trot, the key thing you need to do is relax. The minute you tighten up any part of your body, you will definitely bounce. A key to relaxing is to breathe. After you breathe and relax your body, you will begin to absorb the motion of the trot in your lower back. If you aren't comfortable with the sitting trot, just try a few strides at a time. Sit however you have to to help absorb the bounce. It also helps to learn to sit the trot on a horse whose trot is not too bouncy.

ALERT!

Whenever you feel you are bouncing in the saddle at the trot, take notice of whether you are breathing or not. You would be surprised to learn how many times you are holding your breath when you are riding. Practice breathing deeply and relaxing your entire body. The more you practice it, the more natural it will become when you ride.

Riding the Trot

When you first start to ride the trot, let your horse go just a few trot strides then break back down to the walk. Repeated transitions are a great way to get your horse's back muscles built up, enabling him to carry you better and to feel more comfortable.

This transition also allows you to get back to the walk, where you have become comfortable, before things fall apart. Make use of that old saying "quality not quantity." Getting ten nicely put together trot strides is much better than trotting all the way around the ring but losing a stirrup by the time you are halfway around and bouncing all over the saddle, with the horse reacting to all that by making the trot even more uncomfortable because he is so uncomfortable!

So give yourself some markers along the way—use the dressage letters if they exist or simply pick a post or use cones—and trot halfway to a marker, walk the rest, trot halfway to the next marker, etc. When you feel you have that down well, trot all the way between markers, then walk to the next, and so on. Before you know it, you will be trotting all the way around the ring, but it really doesn't matter how soon this happens. Smoothness matters more, especially to the horse.

FACT

The gait commonly referred to as the "trot" is also known as the "jog" in Western-style riding. The jog is a very slow trot—in the Western Pleasure show ring, the desired speed of the jog is so slow that you might have to look very carefully at the horse's footfalls to even tell that he is trotting at all! While intended to make the horse look "pleasureable" to ride, it tends to look almost painful for a horse's huge body to move that slowly.

Some Trotting Exercises

Doing exercises at the trot will really help you gain your balance and develop a good seat. If you are taking lessons, your instructor will probably have you working at the trot quite a bit.

Counting Steps

As with all the gaits, it can be very informative for you to spend some time concentrating on counting out the steps the horse makes as he trots. Do this on the horse that is the most comfortable to you at the trot. One thing about the trot is that you can pretty easily determine which foot is doing what by glancing down to the huge shoulder blade.

The shoulder moves back as the leg moves forward. If you are going around the arena clockwise, the horse's left side is the "outside," or the one "on the rail." When the left shoulder blade is moving back, the outside front leg is going forward. That means that the right, or inside rear leg is moving forward as well. When those two legs hit the ground, they will shortly be pushing off into the next stride. As they do, you will feel the right hip push up (if you are sitting the trot) so that at that moment you are pushed forward to rise for posting trot, rising just as the outside front leg and inside back are suspended.

Work on feeling these movements. Look down at the shoulder blade as much as you have to but work toward not having to look. Even glancing down can throw your balance off a tad, and chances are you are doing more than just glancing—and the horse certainly feels it.

No Stirrups

You only want to ride with no stirrups at the trot under the best of supervision, on a horse that has a smooth trot, and with whom you are very comfortable. If you are taking lessons, you will most likely do some time trotting without stirrups. It might seem intimidating at first, but you will come to appreciate how much you gain in balance and confidence—how much longer your legs feel and how much better the stirrups feel after you are done with a no-stirrups session!

When you ride with no stirrups in a Western saddle, the stirrups will just flop around since they are pretty well stabilized by the stirrups fenders. Depending on where your stirrups fall on the sides of the horse and how sensitive the horse is to a rider's legs, the stirrups might work against you by flopping against the horse's sides and encouraging him to go faster. You can tie them together using a piece of baling twine. Pass the twine from stirrup to stirrup going under the horse's belly; don't tie it tightly, just enough to be barely taut between the stirrups but not loose enough to hang. Or you can simply slip the stirrups off for the duration of your stirrup-free work. If you don't have a helper to do this for you, you will need to be sure to have a high mounting block to easily get on and off without your stirrups!

If you ride with no stirrups with an English saddle, you will definitely need to restrain the stirrups since the thin stirrups leathers do not stabilize them at all without your feet in them. Keep the stirrups at the ends of the leathers, bring each one up in front of the saddle, and rest it on the horse's opposite shoulder. This gets them out of your way, and they don't weigh enough to bother the horse too much on his shoulders (this can depend on the horse, however—lesson horses are quite accustomed to feeling the stirrups up there).

Ground Poles

Bring out those ground poles again, they are great for doing exercises in any gait, and the trot is no exception. Space them appropriately for the type of trot you are working on (see sidebar on ground pole spacing). You can trot over the poles in succession, or you can trot between two poles to work on straightness at the trot.

ALERT!

When working with ground poles, it's important to space the poles appropriately for the gait you are working at. For the more collected trot, set them approximately 3½ feet apart. For the extended trot, increase the distance between poles to 5 feet. Of course, you might have to adjust a bit if your horse is extremely tall or extremely short.

Flexion

Once your horse is flexing well at the poll while at the walk, you can begin to work on it at the trot. Always have things working well at the walk before trying them at the trot. If something isn't going well in the slower gait, it definitely isn't going to get any better at a faster gait.

Lateral work

Your horse needs to be bending well and responding well to your aids to accomplish lateral work (motion that is sideways not forward, or sideways and forward simultaneously). If you can get some poll flexion and your horse responds well to your leg, start asking for some lateral moves.

The classic lateral move is the "shoulders-in" or "haunches-in" where one end of the horse is slightly off track while still moving forward. Again, you should perfect this at the walk before moving on to the trot.

The Web site *www.funnysnaps.com* shows the four common gaits of the horse—walk, trot, canter, gallop—in a diagram of a moving horse. For the trot, one of the horse's diagonal pairs is outlined in red, making it very easy to see the movement of the legs.

The Extended Trot

When you watch horses loose and see how they move on their own (which you should do as often as you can), you will see them throw their front legs out in an impressive trot stride. In the show ring, this is known as the "extended trot." This is still a two-beat gait, but it's really an exaggeration of your basic trot. A horse can't sustain this gait for long periods of time. But it's a good working gait that you should encourage your horse to move out in after you have mastered the more common trot speed. You will typically have to post a little faster and a bit higher to accommodate this gait, whether you are riding Western or English.

FACT

"Tracking up" is the term used for when the horse's hind foot moves forward and steps into the hoof print of the same side front foot. A horse that is moving out nicely and using his hindquarters will naturally track up. To tell how well your horse tracks up, move him out on a freshly graded surface or videotape him and watch it in slow motion.

▲ In the trot, diagonal legs move at the same time.

Photograph by Cheryl Kimball

The Equitation Show Ring

Pleasure classes are judged on the horse—typically this judging takes place by having the riders simply walk, trot/jog, canter/lope around in circles both clockwise and counterclockwise. When the riders are lined up in the middle at the end of the class, the judge will typically walk down the lineup requesting that each rider back up her horse.

Equitation classes, whether English or Western, are judged on the rider's equitation, as their name implies. They involve a pattern that the rider has to memorize ahead of time and ride perfectly in the class. Equitation classes frequently require the rider to work at the extended trot or jog.

You can work on the regular and extended trot by working them both together. Pick out some markers—fence posts, cones, ground poles, or even from one tree to a boulder, if you are out on a trail that has nice footing. Jog between one post and the next to see how accurately you can time increasing the energy of your body to pick up the extended trot at the right moment. Then slow your horse down to the jog at the next marker you've picked out.

Backing

Although backing is certainly a slower movement than trotting, the horse backs up in the same two-beat motion as the trot. Each diagonal pair of legs goes back at the same time.

Make sure you encourage your horse to pick his legs completely off the ground when he backs. Don't let him get lazy and drag his legs backward. A horse will eventually always come down to the level of his rider, so you need to be sure you are asking the most of him, not letting him be lazy and inaccurate.

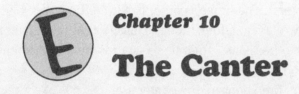

Chapter 10

The Canter

Cantering can be the most fun part of horseback riding. But it can be the most frightening too until you have developed your seat and understand this faster gait better. When you and the horse are in sync, the canter is like covering ground in an easy chair.

What Is the Canter?

A horse's gaits are either "symmetrical," which means the same thing is happening on each side, or asymmetrical, where the legs on each side are not moving the same. The canter is an asymmetrical gait. The canter gait is the fastest of the horse's three basic gaits (the walk and trot were covered in the previous two chapters). The horse's canter is a three-beat gait: one foot hits the ground, then two feet together, then the last foot. Another factor distinguishing it from the other gaits is that there is a moment of suspension, when all four feet are off the ground.

The footfalls for the three beats of the canter are:

1. A hind foot by itself.
2. The other hind foot and its opposite front foot together.
3. The final front foot.
4. There is a moment of suspension when all legs are in the air before the next stride begins.

▲ The canter is the fastest of a horse's three basic gaits.

A "stride" refers to the full cycle of all the footfalls of a particular gait, starting with a hind foot. So one canter stride consists of the three distinct phases of the four legs (two legs move together) and the moment of suspension.

Leads

The canter is a gait about which you will hear the term "leads." A horse is cantering on either a left lead or a right lead. The easiest way to tell which lead the horse is on when watching him move at the canter is to look for the front leg that moves out in front the farthest. The hind leg on the opposite side would have been the original thrust of the canter. So if the horse is on a "right lead," the left hind leg would have pushed off as the first beat in the stride. Then the right hind leg and the left front leg move together, followed by the right front, or leading leg, which stretches out in front farther than the other front leg did. Of course, the opposite occurs on the left lead.

The Natural Lead

Horses naturally balance themselves—they are exceptionally good at putting their feet where they need to be to keep that big body above ground. So when a horse is cantering in a clockwise direction, it's natural for him to be on his right lead, allowing for a better balance in the direction of the clockwise curve.

Cross Cantering

When a horse takes off on a hind leg but does not follow the canter sequence of footfalls, it's referred to as cross cantering. This could be dangerous for both you and the horse. He could easily strike a front foot with a hind or simply get off balance and fall. You can almost immediately feel this awkward and jerky movement.

Counter Cantering

Counter cantering is when the horse takes up the lead opposite from the natural lead he should take considering the direction he is going. So a left lead while cantering clockwise is considered a "counter canter." This is sometimes used intentionally to build up muscles and balance in a young or developing horse. Later in this chapter, you will learn how to request the canter from your horse, and therefore how you would request the counter canter.

Observing the Canter

As with the walk and the trot, it helps you to watch horses move on their own to understand the canter and how to ride it.

Loose Horses

Loose horses travel so smoothly and naturally that it's important to watch them whenever you get the opportunity. You will see the purest movement the horse has to offer without the impediment of trying to balance a 130-pound vertically oriented human on his back. Try to watch horses in a place with great footing, like an indoor or outdoor arena. Then you can watch the horses moving freely without concern for rocks and other obstacles.

Watch which legs move when. Concentrate on one leg at a time so you can focus on the movement—you'll find that it's pretty hard to watch two or more legs at once. Watch the shoulder and hip, two areas of movement that greatly impact how you move in the saddle. Also watch what the horses do with their heads at each gait. Once you really appreciate watching horses while they are loose, watch them do everything on their own—go over ground poles and cavelettis and over jumps. It's probably hard to get a horse to do a barrel pattern on his own, but a frisky horse running around on his own will cut plenty of sharp corners!

FACT

In Western riding, the canter is referred to as the "lope." And the point that the horse steps off with his hind leg into the canter is referred to mostly by English riders as the "canter depart."

Longeing

"Longeing" is when you clip a 30-foot long lead rope to the horse's halter and work him in circles around you. Longeing is a tool used to exercise a horse when you can't ride him. It can be a useful tool for starting to get an out-of-shape horse in condition or to slowly start an injured horse back into an exercise regimen.

Going around and around in circles can be extremely boring for a horse, so it's important for the horse's mental well being to use longeing only as a means to an end. When you need to longe your horse, break things up with lots of gait transitions and changes of direction.

Get an experienced horseperson to give you a lesson or two in longeing horses. You'll want to know some techniques and some safety factors. It's always best to longe a horse in an enclosed area—you don't want him accidentally running loose with a 30-foot rope attached. Never wrap the longe line around your arm or hand. A horse could pick up quite a head of steam on the longe line, and you don't want to be securely attached to it!

It's common to use a longe whip. Of course, you have taught your horse to be respectful and responsive (or bought one that is and learned how to maintain that respect and responsiveness), so you won't need to use the whip to defend yourself! (Don't laugh, many people have to do just that.) The whip can be used as a long-distance aid to help encourage the horse up into the next gait. Never hit the horse with the whip—swish it around on the ground, flap it in the air, or give it a crack in the air if you have to. If he is constantly moving in on you, you can hold the whip straight out in front of you and let him run into the end of it himself so that he gets the message to stay out on the circle.

As for form, always ask the horse to carry his head and body in an arc in the shape of the circle in the direction he is moving. You don't want him to carry his head to the outside, counter to the direction he is going in—that won't be conducive to developing proper gait movements. This happens a lot and makes the longe line a great place for a horse to learn to brace against pressure, something you prefer not to happen. If he carries his head to the outside, keep bumping him by pulling in slightly on the line, stopping immediately when his head is in proper position. You might have to do this several times to get your message across, especially if the horse has been longed many times by someone who didn't pay attention to this.

You can use the longe to teach a horse voice commands, which can help if you are inexperienced and your horse is inexperienced. Voice commands allow you to change gaits despite your position! Of course, good position and appropriate use of the aids that develop communication via feel are your goals, but voice commands can help you get there.

Finally, longeing a horse can be an excellent way to really pay attention to how his body moves at the different gaits. Even better might be to watch someone else longe (or ride) a horse. Either way, you are obviously in better viewing position than when you are on his back. And while longeing, you can control his movements so you can quickly compare what happens in the different gaits.

FACT

A good way to condition a horse on a longe line is to ask him to change gaits often. Always start out at a walk to let your horse know that being longed isn't just about racing around in circles. End at a walk to cool him down if he gets a good workout. Give him lots of breaks where he can stretch his neck out. But in between ask for a lot of up and down transitions—walk-trot, trot-walk, trot-canter, canter-trot—all the time watching his body while you are longeing to learn more about his movements.

Riding the Canter

Perhaps one of the most difficult aspects of riding the canter gait smoothly involves the speed factor. Beginning riders often get tense and hold their breath because they become fearful at this faster pace. Tensing and holding your breath, which could bounce you out of the saddle at a dead walk, gets exaggerated at the canter.

Holding your breath increases the tenseness of your body. When your body is tense, instead of being able to go with the motion of the horse, you will stiffly pound up and down in the saddle. Then you'll lose a stirrup. And even worse, such stiffness and bouncing will cause you to grip with your knees and probably bend forward in the saddle—both of which will cause most horses to increase their speed. It's a vicious cycle!

If you are a novice rider, this is another place in which riding that "broke-to-death" horse will work in your favor. Learn to canter on a horse that can immediately pick up the cue—the more you have to do to get a horse to canter, the more you will lose your posture and seat position. The horse that is well experienced will also be able to accommodate your less-than-perfect balance and seat. And the more time you can spend cantering on a horse like this, the faster you will develop your seat and learn to move with his movements.

Some riders are so fearful of cantering, they don't get out of the trot for years. It's best to perfect your seat at one gait before moving up to a faster one. But you will never become comfortable cantering unless you practice.

The Rider's Hips

The rider's hips and pelvis are the focus of movement when riding the canter. You need to relax your hips and your pelvis needs to be able to easily and fluidly rock forward and back with a "scooping" motion in between to move with the horse's movement. If this is a problem for you, look for Feldenkrais, yoga, tai chi, or some other type of exercise that focus on the pelvis area.

While the trot is a clear two-beat rhythm, when you canter, you can feel a three-beat rhythm. Count "one-two-three" to yourself as you canter. You can even practice while sitting in your dining room chair (although this is best while eating alone, or your family might wonder what is wrong with you!).

If your horse's movements aren't going right, stop and start again. In fact, stopping and starting a lot can be valuable. Ride just a few canter strides at a time, coming down to a trot before you get disorganized. It's better to keep smooth and do smooth downward transitions than to canter longer. Increase the length of your canter time as you get more comfortable.

The Canter Cues

For a horse to pick up the canter, he has to move his hip toward the lead you want to take and move his shoulder away.

Leg Aids

If you are going in a clockwise circle (i.e., to the right), the horse needs to push off into the canter with his left hind leg. So one canter cue is to put your outside (left) leg behind the girth area to encourage him to put his left hind leg more underneath him. At the same time, you can hold the inside (right) leg lightly against his side and steady your reins against his neck to help move his shoulder toward the outside to give him ample space to reach with his inside front, or leading, leg.

Your Seat

A goal for getting a horse to canter is to be able to use just your seat as a cue. This is where your one-two-three rhythm really helps. You can begin to move your seat in the canter rhythm and, since horses are always looking to be as comfortable as possible, they will follow along with that feel. Of course, if a horse has been ridden by many unskilled riders, they often have become dull to this kind of sensitivity and don't care if you are pounding around up there begging them to canter. And some are so keyed in to other cues—crops, clucks, and voice commands—that they aren't paying attention to your seat.

Other Cues

There is nothing wrong with using clucks, crops, or other cues to get your horse to canter. If this is what the horse is used to, then by all means use the cues. But the idea of good horsemanship is to always work toward making your cues as subtle as possible. Sometimes for some horses at a stage in their education "as subtle as possible" is a good thwack with the crop. But to work toward something truly subtle, you need to always ask first with the cue that you would *like* to use to get your horse to canter. Then follow through with what it takes to have him canter. All the while, never forget your responsibility to learn what your body position should be to help him get to the canter.

What is "neck reining"?

The term "neck reining" refers to holding the reins with one hand and having your horse move off the reins by laying them on one side of his neck. Neck reining is typically a Western-style technique, almost always used when riding with a leveraged, nonjointed bit also called a "curb" bit. English riders do not use neck reining, they always (well, almost always) ride with two hands. And young horses in training will be ridden with two hands until they understand enough to be able to be taught neck reining.

Canter Exercises

Interestingly, some of the most useful exercises to help with the canter do not need to be done at the canter gait at all! Exercises that help a horse with lateral movement are great for preparing for the canter since, as we learned above, the horse needs to move his hip and his shoulder laterally to easily pick up the canter stride.

Leg Yields

The "leg yield" is an exercise where you request your horse to step sideways while keeping his body straight and maintaining forward movement. So, depending on the amount that he steps in the sideways direction, you could start at the lower left corner of the arena and move forward and laterally, ending up in the right upper corner of the arena. You should be able to accomplish this with a soft but firm, steady but not heavy pressure from the leg and rein opposite of the direction you want to travel.

So if you want to move laterally to the right, offer a little pressure on your left leg and reins; take pressure off your right leg and rein to open up that side and give him the feeling that he has a place to go. Forward and straight is the key—if he moves just a tiny bit laterally, praise him, walk out, and try again.

You'll soon be adding several strides until you can make that whole trip from one corner of the arena to the opposite one. And, again, if the horse you usually ride is just learning this movement, to know what this movement should feel like, you could find it helpful to ride another, more experienced horse that knows how to leg yield. Leg yielding is mostly a building block to higher level lateral movements, so once you and your horse have it down, you may not use it much after that.

ALERT!

Straightness of form reigns supreme in riding. Commonly, you will see a horse bent in the rear with the circle and with his head turned to the outside. Even when you are riding your horse in a fairly tight circle, he should be straight; his spine should align along a straight path mirroring the arc of the circle.

Shoulders-In

Ride your horse down the rail and move his shoulders off the "track" and toward the inside of the ring while his hindquarters remain on the track. This is "shoulders-in." A responsive horse going clockwise (to the right) should be able to respond to slight pressure from your inside leg to keep his haunches on the rail and slight pressure from your outside leg and outside rein to move his shoulders in. If your horse hasn't done much of this, don't expect or even ask him to hold this for several strides. Take your success in small bits—go a step or two, praise him, straighten out, and walk out a little, then try again.

Haunches-In

The opposite of shoulders-in, haunches-in is asking your horse to step his hindquarters off the straight track and toward the middle while keeping his shoulders on track. Do this by applying slight pressure in the opposite way for shoulders-in. If you are going clockwise (to the right), apply pressure slightly behind the girth with your outside leg and at the girth with your inside leg with help from your reins to keep his shoulders on the rail.

Both haunches-in and shoulders-in help your horse move his body laterally at your request to be in the proper position to easily pick up the canter.

FACT

Don't be fooled by a big Western saddle into thinking the horse can't feel your seat between all that leather, wool lining, and saddle pad. Although the horse might not be able to feel the points in your seat bones like sharp knives as he might if you were riding bareback, he can definitely feel the difference in where your weight is and the differing pressures of your seat bones.

You can do both shoulders-in and haunches-in at the trot after you have perfected them at the walk. But don't move up to the faster gait unless you feel very confident at the walk—a faster gait will only exaggerate inaccuracies.

Cantering

Cantering itself is, of course, a great exercise for learning to canter. But don't just rip around the ring. Learn to control the speed and cadence of the canter. Slow it down, then speed it up. Help your horse learn what speed you want, not just by hauling back on his mouth, but by using your seat as much as your hands. In other words, move in the saddle in the speed you want him to be in. As always, horses are looking for the comfort zone. If you are sitting well and not pounding on his back (which might make him speed up no matter what you want!), then he will try to figure out what speed to be at to match the feel of your seat.

Galloping

While many riders don't have much interest or need for the gallop—the same stride as the canter with greater speed in the form of quicker strides and longer suspension—it can be important to ride the gallop from time to time. First, it allows you to realize that you can. It also allows the horse to know he can. But don't gallop until you feel extremely confident in all other gaits. And even then, do it on Old Faithful (if he can still muster up a gallop!).

ALERT!

A great way to sour your horse is to overdo. As with any new thing you teach your horse, stay on this side of success. Don't drill him. Get a couple of strides of a lateral movement, and move on to some other work. Then ask again. Once you consistently receive an immediate response to your request, hold the movement a little longer. Before you know it, you will go all around the ring doing whatever exercise you ask on a horse that is happy to comply because he has been allowed to understand your requests.

At the gallop, it can be helpful to get into "two-point position" in which you raise your seat out of the saddle. Moving with the fast motion of the gallop can be almost impossible without raising your seat. However, once again, Old Faithful comes in handy—it would be particularly unfortunate for a horse to spook while you were going so fast and already up out of the saddle!

It helps to learn to gallop in the arena rather than out on the trails—if the horse gets frightened at the gallop and takes off uncontrollably, at least in the arena there's really no where he could go. Also someone could help slow him down.

Young horses and those who don't go at great speeds a lot—either they aren't ridden fast or don't have a lot of free space to run fast on their own—can get scared at the gallop. If you watch horses on their own, when galloping, they often stop to kick up their heels. They, of course, feel good, and they can get up enough speed to frighten themselves! So again, start with Old Faithful, be sure you have the previous gait going well and that your horse is with you, so you can rein him in before things get out of hand.

Cantering on the trail is different from cantering in an enclosed arena. Sometimes it's easier—a tree-lined trail can allow you to forget about steering and concentrate on your position. Some horses and riders are more comfortable cantering on the trail than having to maneuver all the corners —and possible breaks in stride—that an arena presents. But if you are trail riding with others, be aware that horses have a tendency to like to race each other—a canter can become an uncontrollable gallop pretty quickly.

Chapter 11
The Natural Aids

The things you use to communicate with your horse are called "aids." There are several aids that are part of your body that are called "natural aids." These are your hands, legs, and seat. Your voice can also be a natural aid. Artificial aids, which we will cover in the next chapter, are equipment like bits, crops, quirts, dressage whips, and spurs. These artificial aids can sound harsh but they all, if used appropriately, can be helpful tools in being effective with your horse. It's how they are used, not what they are.

Hands

Your hands are a major means of communication between you and your horse. A horse can learn a lot about you simply from how you touch him. And when you ride, your hands are holding the reins that are attached to a piece of metal in the horse's mouth. You can see why a horse appreciates a rider who has what is known as "light hands," "soft hands," or "good hands."

Think of the Horse

When you pick up on your horse's reins, do it with respect. Remember that there is a piece of metal in his mouth. Learn not to be abrupt in anything you do with the horse—to the horse, abruptness is harsh. But you also don't want to tiptoe around the horse and seem "sneaky." You want to be smooth.

Of course, everyone has to learn, and you might be less than smooth in your handling of the horse at first; this is where it becomes clear why beginners should learn about horses and how to ride from a more experienced mount. The well trained horse knows how good things can be, and he can be quite forgiving of an inexperienced horse person. You can be less smooth with things like putting his tack on, and he won't get all upset about it. Young horses don't have the experience to know that everything will work out all right; they need to have more experienced handlers and riders who know how to give horses some additional confidence.

As you gain more experience, you will learn smoothness. You'll learn how put the horse's tack on efficiently as you do it more often, and you'll learn how to get on without being abrupt. And when you mount up and are ready to pick up the reins and go, you'll begin to pick them up with some finesse. Always adjust the reins to the length you want before you ride off, so you aren't reeling them in fast and furiously while trying to catch up with your horse.

Contact

Different instructors will advise you differently concerning how much "contact" they want you to have between the reins and your horse's mouth. "Light contact" means there is a droop in the reins along the horse's neck.

"Full contact" would be when the reins are taut between your hands and the horse's mouth to the point where the horse might even be bending his head and arching his neck. There is a time and place for both types of contact.

Horses can learn to be okay about riding with full contact for a period of time. But when you are schooling a horse and keeping him in full contact for long periods of time, be sure to take breaks once in a while. To clear his airways along that long neck, a horse needs to drop his head. And it helps him relax and stretch his back muscles when you give him a break from contact periodically during a schooling session or lesson.

FACT

When the reins are taut, you have full contact with the bit, and the horse's face forms a vertical line perpendicular to the ground, it's referred to in some disciplines as being "on the bit." If the horse's face is tilted at all back toward his chest, he is referred to as being "behind the bit."

The Hand Brake

As you will read later, the reins/bit combination is not the only tool for stopping a horse. They are a piece of the braking puzzle, for sure, but well trained horses do not need their mouths pulled off to stop. You will be able to use your seat and the energy in your body to help slow the horse down and come to a stop. Some horses have been taught to really plant their feet the minute the rider's seat is heavy in the saddle. Watch out when riding those horses, if you aren't alert you could easily be launched over the horse's head!

When you want your horse to stop, you will probably pick up on the reins and pull back as part of the stopping cue. Pull back only as far as you need to get your horse to stop. When he is just about to come to a full stop, release the reins to let him know that stopping is exactly what you want him to do. If you continue to pull even after he's stopped, the horse will be getting one of those frustrating mixed messages—"I stopped, but she is still pulling on me. Maybe she didn't want me to stop, so I'll keep going. Oh no, she's still pulling, and now she's getting mad . . . ."

If you pull back on both reins, a horse should give to you at the head and neck. A horse that has not been taught to give in this manner, also referred to as "yielding," will brace against the pull of both reins and have his head up in the air. If such a horse begins to run away with you, you will have quickly lost control. In this case, never pull back on both reins, pull on one, then the other, back and forth, until you feel the horse begin to slow. Getting the horse slightly off a straight line can help break the impulsion in his hind-quarters. Of course, your own horse will be taught never to do such a thing, but when you are riding other people's horses, you just never know!

ALERT!

Since runaway horses can be a common experience with beginners riding other people's horses, we'll cover one more detail: if a horse has not been taught to yield to the bit, pulling on one rein and trying to stop him by stopping the impulsion will not work. And on top of that, it can be more dangerous than the runaway situation to begin with! A horse can run fast with his head sideways—and he can fall down easily too.

Different Bits

As you recall from Chapter 3, there are many different kinds of bits that are used in riding horses. While some people will advocate a curb style bit with a higher port and more leverage for the beginning rider, it's certainly fairer to the horse to use a gentler bit that doesn't hurt when operated by unskilled hands. Contrary to popular belief, it's more appropriate to use a more leveraged bit on an educated horse ridden by an experienced rider than vice versa.

ESSENTIAL

While we are on the subject of hands, riding and horse-related activities—lifting bales of hay, carrying full water buckets, replacing broken fence boards, grooming a horse—can take a toll on your hands. Wear gloves as often as possible, especially in cold temperatures. Keep moisturizer in your tack box or use it on the way out the door of your house. Keep a supply of moisturized hand wipes in your tack box and vehicle as well.

An Exercise

An interesting thing to do to learn a little bit about how your hands feel to the horse and to understand the importance of improving your timing is to feel the bridle yourself. Get a bridle and a partner (it helps if one of you is a more experienced rider). Hold the bridle in your hands at the bit. You are the horse. Your partner is the rider. She stands behind you and works the reins. As she pulls on the reins at different amounts of contact, you'll feel how the bit feels and understand how much pressure you are putting on the bit when you pull back on the reins. But, even more important, every so often you, the horse, should give to the rider's pull by dipping your hands toward yourself. The rider can improve her timing for releasing the pressure at the split second the horse gives to her.

You can certainly do this exercise on horseback, and you will, but it helps to play around with it before subjecting your horse (i.e., his sensitive mouth) to it. And with some horses that have not been taught to yield to the pressure of the bit, you can stand there all day and wait for a release! As a human guinea pig, you'll feel the release repeatedly. And with that experience, you might even find that your "unyielding" horse is actually giving a tiny bit, perhaps as much as he can at the moment until he learns more about yielding. Until you did this two-person exercise, you didn't even feel the slight give that your horse was offering!

The Rider's Legs

A second significant set of aids is your legs. Both legs are sometimes used together, sometimes each leg is used separately. The horse knows every move your legs make, and he is aware of everything going on that has to do with him at all times. Therefore it's important to learn to use your legs with purpose.

How Close?

There are a couple of schools of thought about how much contact your legs should have on the horse's side. Some riders like to give the horse a gentle hug with their legs—not tight, but enough so he feels it; and others like to have lots of air between them and the horse. And some like a position in between. If you are taking instruction, you will, of course, want to do what your instructor tells you. If you don't agree, then you might want to find different instruction.

Some disciplines require riders to be closer at the leg than others. In dressage or reining, for instance, being close to the horse helps you with accuracy and immediacy of your cues. But with hunters/jumpers and those riding young horses, you might find that having some distance between your legs and your horse's sides makes it easier for the horse to jump, or, makes the youngster less claustrophobic.

FACT

In some English riding lessons, you will ride with color-coded reins. The braided reins have blue, yellow, and red areas that allow the instructor to give you a quick direction about how much contact to have—e.g., "tighten the reins up to the green area." When you loosen up the rein entirely and evenly on each side and let your horse stretch his neck way out and relax, it's known as "riding on the buckle" since English reins are usually connected in the center by a buckle.

Dullness

You bump your horse in the sides. He doesn't go anywhere. You bump him again. He still doesn't go anywhere. Finally you give him a pretty good double thump, and he drifts off like he has the rest of the day to go no further than the other side of the arena. And once he starts going, you still are bumping him with your legs. This scenario will make a horse dull to your legs in just about three rides.

There are lots of critical details to riding horses successfully, but being effective when using your legs is one of the most important. There is nothing more frustrating or more ridiculous looking than someone thumping and thumping her horse with her legs and nothing is happening. Your legs will wear out pretty fast.

But if the horse moves, and you keep thumping, what message are you sending him? Horses are pretty simple—you bump your legs, they move, you stop bumping. Okay, so the next time you bump your legs, the horse moves because he remembers that is what got you to stop bumping his sides the last time. But if you don't stop bumping when he moves, what does he think? I move when she bumps, but she keeps bumping. I'm really not sure what I am supposed to do. So you know what, I'll just do nothing.

And so your horse tunes out your legs. And you've just lost one of your most important aids.

ALERT!

School horses often go into a sort of "zone" while they are being ridden for a lesson. They are subject to so many different riders with such varied abilities that they never receive consistent cues and releases. What would happen to you if you got mixed messages all the time? You would either get frustrated (this kind of horse does not make a good school horse because he "acts up" when he gets frustrated) or you would tune out all of it. The horse that can tune out all of it makes a good school horse. And that is where voice commands come in handy, because they are rarely inconsistent.

Leg Cues

Here are a few possible cues you might want to use your legs for:

- Squeeze slightly or bump your heels to ask your horse to move. As soon as possible after the horse moves, stop your leg movement. As you get more skilled, you will ease off when you just begin to feel the horse shift his weight to move. But as you get more experienced, you won't need your legs to move your horse, you will do it with your seat and the body energy you give off. In the beginning, though, you will probably use your legs a lot.
- Even pressure from the entire part of one leg against your horse's side along with the pressure of the rein on the same side along the horse's neck is a cue to step his whole body sideways in a lateral move called a sidepass.

- Move one leg back an inch or two and turn your heel into the horse's side: you want the horse to step the hind leg on that side over. Keep the reins in neutral to indicate to him that you want just his hind leg to move, his front legs should stay where they are.
- Have some contact on the bit with the horse yielding ever so slightly, move one leg ahead a couple of inches toward the shoulder, lay pressure from the rein on the same side on the horse's neck and ask the front quarters to step away from the pressure.

If you have never done these things while sitting on a horse's back, or if your horse has never had anyone request things in this manner, you will need to practice until he understands what you want and you are better at communicating it.

What Not to Do with Your Legs

One thing you don't want to do with your legs is grip them to hang on. Beginning riders might wonder how they will stay on the horse; you will learn to develop your balance and weight in the saddle for this purpose. (Don't worry, more on both of those coming up!) Gripping with your legs can be disconcerting to any horse and works to your disadvantage when the horse is out of control, such as running too fast. Gripping hard with your legs to stay on a fast moving horse can cause the horse to add bucking to the adventure, something you don't want. It's best to avoid learning this habit, it isn't useful to riding.

ESSENTIAL

Your aids can be made to be more effective by wearing apparel designed for riding horses. For example, full height boots with an English saddle can help your leg be more steady and more effective. English saddles have thin leathers extending down to the stirrup, unlike Western saddles that have a wide leather piece known as a "fender" under your leg. Also, gloves can help your hands be more effective, but use gloves designed for riding—others can be slippery.

Your Seat

The use of your seat and weight in the saddle can take the beginning rider the most time to develop to her advantage. Once you learn to use the seat, you can give the horse cues that are almost imperceptible to someone watching. And you will be safer riding if you are sitting deeply weighted in the saddle.

Seat Bones

The prominent pelvic bones that stick down when you sit are referred to as the "seat bones." The horse can feel these even through a saddle pad, the leather, tree, and stuffing of the saddle. You can weight one or the other seat bone and that frees up the horse's back on the unweighted side and allows for freer movement in that direction.

> Softness does not mean wimpy! Even those riders whose hands are especially light do firm up on their horses when it's necessary. The key to success with horses is being effective—sometimes firming up on the reins is what it takes to effectively achieve whatever you're trying to achieve. But it isn't with malice or anger that you get firm—it's with sureness, confidence, and for the purpose of clarity.

Gain Weight

Try to move your ten-pound cat off your bed in the middle of the night, and you know how living thing can make itself heavier—suddenly that cat seems to weigh a twenty-five pounds, and she isn't going anywhere! You can do the same with your weight in the saddle. Sit back and push your weight into your seat bones, and you can stay pretty well seated while the horse is moving. If you sit lightly and just perch yourself up there, you are already halfway off if the horse moves quickly.

Breathing

To use your seat and seat bones accurately and adequately, you need to breathe. Holding your breath keeps your weight a bit elevated. Breathing deeply and regularly helps you to deepen your seat and to maintain the balance you need to ride well.

Voice Commands

Voice commands are words that you teach your horse to know, the same as you would teach your dog to understand the words "sit," "bark," or "roll over." Commonly, voice commands are taught to horses during their early training, especially by trainers who use longeing (exercising a horse in circles around you at the end of a 30-foot line). Horses commonly learn the gaits ("walk," "trot," and "canter") in a specific tone and emphasis ("waaaaalk," "trot!" and "cannnn-ter!" are typical).

Another word commonly taught, which can be quite useful for beginning riders, is "Whoa!" This word can be pronounced either "Woe" or "Hoe," so you might want to know which way your horse has been taught; he probably will get it if you pronounce it either way, but since this word is often used for emergencies, you're safest if you know for certain.

E ALERT!

Don't rely completely on voice commands if the situation gets out of control with your horse! Use every aid at your disposal. If a horse is running away with you, pull on one rein, then the other. Sit back deep in your seat (perhaps the hardest of all). Don't grip with your feet, this spurs the horse on whether you have spurs on or not! Breathe, which will help you sit back and get deep in the saddle. Command "Whoa!" but don't scream at the horse, this just adds to the chaos and might serve to get him more wound up.

Teaching a horse to respond to voice commands is a matter of training preference. When you take lessons on a school horse that has learned voice commands, your instructor will spell the words so that your horse doesn't change gaits on her cue, not yours. Riding a horse that knows voice commands, however, can be useful for a beginning rider. The beginner doesn't yet have the feel or timing of her other aids to be effective in her requests for changes of gait. You can work on getting your cues perfected while at the same time saying "trot" so that the horse will move out.

Riders at high levels of horsemanship do not tend to use voice commands. They certainly aren't appropriate in competition. Accomplished riders rely on their skill in using their other natural aids to communicate with their horse. After all, even when a horse can understand simple words, he does not understand the English language. But the horse does understand the feel of the rider's body, since feel is the horse's language. (More about the concept of "feel" to come in Chapter 13.)

No One Said It Would Be Easy

The natural aids can be the hardest of all things to learn to use effectively with your horse. Not only does the horse need to be clued in on what you mean—i.e., "trained"—but you have to sort out the movement of individual parts of your body usually separately from other parts. You need to move your foot without moving your leg, to move your head without moving your body, to drop your shoulder back (which changes your balance and the weight in your seat) without moving your head. Maybe it would help to practice simultaneously rubbing your stomach and patting your head before you ever get on a horse!

Chapter 12

Artificial Aids

Subtle use of natural aids—hands, legs, and seat—is always the goal for the accomplished horseback rider. But for some riders, some horses, and some combinations of horse and rider, artificial aids such as a crop or spurs are necessary. And the bit, considered an essential by most riders, is also an artificial aid.

Why Artificial Aids?

Horses are, by nature, what humans might call lazy. However, think about the horse's natural life: they move to find food or water or to escape perceived danger. Those three objectives alone keep them moving quite a lot of the time. The rest of the time, an animal the size of a horse needs to conserve his energy. Food in the wild is not always plentiful or reliable, and the horse never knows when he is going to have to burn off some calories escaping a lion, tiger, or bear.

In comes the person expecting her horse to pack her around for a couple of hours. Not only that, but often it's in the environment of a rectangular ring or an indoor arena with walls on all sides. This cannot make much sense to a horse to begin with. And then consider the fact that humans are mostly inaccurate with our timing and inconsistent at best with our requests. So that the horse might need some encouragement in the form of artificial aids to ride them really shouldn't come as a big surprise.

FACT

Horse shows and other competitive equestrian events have some rules regarding bits. For instance, in Western classes snaffle bits are often okay for showing horses up until they are five years old but after that, you are expected to use a curb bit. Check the rules before you compete. Allow time to get your horse used to a new bit if the event you plan to ride in requires you to use something different from your usual bit.

The Bit

The most common artificial aid is the bit. The bit has been around almost as long as the horse has been ridden instead of eaten for dinner. In fact, archaeological studies in Eurasia are beginning to show evidence that humans might have been riding horses with bridles and bits as early as 4000 B.C.

While practically synonymous with horseback riding, the bit is also quite controversial. It's pretty easy to understand the controversy when you think about the fact that a bit is a large piece of metal that sits in the horse's tender mouth.

The Snaffle Bit

A snaffle bit is one of the most simple and least harsh bits. It's highly recommended as the best bit to train a horse. The lack of leverage and harshness allows the young horse to think about the rider and what the rider is asking of him, rather than simply focusing on the thing in his mouth. The snaffle bit has a joint in the middle that gives when the rider pulls back on the reins. It can be connected at the sides by either round rings (known as an O-ring snaffle) or D-shaped rings (known as a D-ring snaffle). There are other bits with jointed mouthpieces that are commonly referred to as snaffle bits, but if the bit has "shanks" on the sides, they make the bit a leveraged one, not a snaffle bit.

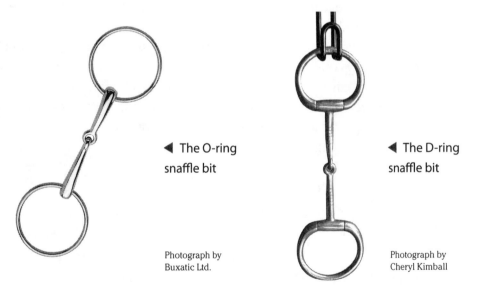

◀ The O-ring
snaffle bit

◀ The D-ring
snaffle bit

Photograph by
Buxatic Ltd.

Photograph by
Cheryl Kimball

The snaffle bit has a leather piece that runs from ring to ring and under the horse's chin. The leather strap is for no other reason than to prevent one side of the bit from pulling through the horse's mouth if you pull on just one rein from the other side.

The domestication of horses represents a well documented area of human history. For some interesting information on how horses became so important to humans, visit the International Museum of the Horse Web site at *www.imh.org*.

FACT

Leveraged Bits

Bits that have long pieces of metal on the sides (called "shanks") operate using leverage. When you pull back on the reins, you move the lever, and it exerts pressure on the horse's mouth. The mouthpiece is typically not jointed—it can either be a straight piece of metal or, more likely, the mouthpiece has a bend in it known as a "port." If you remember your high school physics, the longer the lever, the more pressure it can exert. The higher the port, the more it affects the horse's mouth. These bits collectively are known as "curb bits."

Curb bits usually have a chin strap called a "curb chain" that, unlike the strap on a snaffle bit that simply prevents the bit from pulling through the mouth, the curb chain puts added pressure on the horses chin.

You can see where this would not be a good bit to educate a young horse. It's exerting pressure from a couple of different directions, which can be quite distracting. And it simply can be quite harsh in hands that are not well educated.

Which Bit?

A common way of thinking about the bit is that the less control you have over your horse, the harsher the bit you need. Or the greener the rider, the more control she needs over her horse, so she should use a curb bit. This is completely opposite from what is best for the horse.

A green rider or a green horse (which is best not combined!) should use the least harsh bit possible. Until the rider develops good hands and learns how to use the bit to her advantage, it's best to not subject the horse to inconsistent handling of his mouth. Even the most educated horse that is quite accustomed to a curb style bit will become frustrated having his mouth jerked on by an inexperienced rider.

The more experienced rider can make a lot of use of the curb bit. A horse can be more responsive to the curb bit, and the experienced rider can get a lot out of that. As a new rider, you will probably want to learn on an experienced horse that is not dull to the snaffle bit.

The best thing you can do is to learn how to ride with light, soft hands. Avoid relying only on the bit for control of your horse. A horse you ride should be so well halter broke by then that you shouldn't even be thinking about using the bit for control, but simply as a means of communication. Learning how to effectively use all your natural aids—legs, hands, and seat—will put you in a better position to use the bit to your advantage.

Many trainers give young horses their first couple of rides using just a halter. If the horse has been well halter broke, this is going to be as effective as a bit at this stage anyway. The young horse has enough to think about with a saddle and rider; he doesn't need a bit thrown into the mix.

Changing Bits

Your horse's trainer or your riding instructor might suggest changing the bit you are using on your horse or the horse you are riding. If you are riding a lesson horse, the bit choice is up to the instructor. But if it's your own horse, become knowledgeable about bits so you can make an informed decision and speak authoritatively about it with your trainer or instructor. Don't just change bits without having a clear reason and a clear understanding of what you are trying to accomplish. And always investigate whether you can accomplish what you are trying to do simply through increasing your horsemanship skills rather than equipment changes.

Many times when a new bit (or any new piece of equipment) is put in your horse's mouth, the change in the horse seems miraculous. But two weeks down the road, you'll find yourself back where you were before the bit was changed. This is a clear indication that you need to concentrate on your riding skills. What has probably happened is that the horse has become dull to the new piece of equipment, just like he did to the old bit that you thought you needed to change. It's *you* that needs to change. Your horsemanship, not the equipment, is the important part.

ALERT!

There is a school of thought that the bridle needs to be adjusted so that the bit sits high enough in the horse's mouth to cause two or three wrinkles in the corner of the mouth. To those who are really looking to refine their horsemanship, however, a bit this high is putting constant unreleased pressure on the horse. Strive to use even less pressure to communicate with your horse. Why use the pressure of those two wrinkles before you even pick up on the reins?

Crops and Whips

English riders are often seen carrying either a short stubby stick with a flat piece of leather on the end, known as a crop, or a thin whip around 2½ feet in length. These tools are used to tap the horse on the rump to encourage him to move out.

The well-trained horse who has learned to respond, and not been made dull, to the rider's leg will not need these tools. Many lesson horses, which have had to tune out the inconsistency of different riders requests, need the rider to carry a crop or whip. Western riders can use these tools in the training or lesson ring but it isn't appropriate to carry them into the Western show ring. Western riders rely more on the traditional cowboy "spur" or something called a "quirt" for this kind of encouragement. English riders use spurs as well. Spurs are explained later.

ALERT!

You can carry a dressage whip in the dressage test ring. Never hold the whip in the hand you will salute the judge with! Hold it in the hand that you will keep on the reins.

Why a Crop?

If you are riding a horse that has become dull to the rider's leg, you will very quickly tire from bumping on the horse's sides to get him to go or pick up the pace. He has learned to tune bumping out because his experience has been that sometimes it means something, sometimes it doesn't.

A well-timed tap with the crop is all some horses need. But if they have been made dull to the crop, you can feel like you have to beat on him (don't!) to get him to even acknowledge you have a crop in your hand. If you are looking at a horse like this for purchase, and you are a beginner, you might want to reconsider. On the other hand, this kind of horse will demand that you improve your horsemanship because he isn't giving anything that doesn't hold meaning to him—and fewer and fewer things hold meaning to him over the years.

ESSENTIAL

Learn to use a crop or whip with finesse. A crop is short and requires a little more arm movement to use. A whip is longer and can be used easier with your arm in place but it also has a lot more sting so be careful how you use it! Your goal is for your horse to respect your aids—artificial or natural—you don't want your horse to be afraid.

Dressage whips operate on the same principle but they are longer and can be easier for the inexperienced rider to use because they can reach the horse's rump easier. However, dressage whips can also sting pretty badly so practice tapping with it before you get on! Your horse might not appreciate your using him for whipping practice, and you might get some responses you don't want, like bolting or kicking out.

Quirts

Quirts are wide, flat pieces of leather with a handle on one end used in Western riding like a crop is used in English riding. You might see riders give their horses big whacks on the rump as the team heads for home after running barrels. While it's rather crude use of a quirt, the flat leather does have less of a sting than a whip.

Spurs

Spurs aren't terribly large pieces of equipment, but they can be complicated! The end of the spur that spins around is called a "rowel." The rowel has different numbers of points on it. Because rowels can catch the ends of your chaps, they sometimes have small metal protrusions on top called "chap guards." The metal sides that wrap around your boot are called "heel bands," and can be intricately engraved. Spurs are held on with straps that attach to the spur on a small button called a "strap pin." The rod that protrudes from the back of the heel band and ends in the rowel is called the "shank," which can be short or of considerable length.

If you don't have "quiet legs," forget about spurs for now. You will not be happy with the results of accidentally bumping an extremely sensitive horse with a spur! And if you tend to clamp with your legs when the horse underneath you goes too fast, forget about spurs for now as well—that is a rodeo in the making. Don't use spurs until you have control of your legs and seat.

Once you have quiet legs and a reasonably good seat, spurs are fine. As with anything, it's all in how you use them. Spurs are not for hurting your horse. They are simply to back up your leg. And, as discussed below, if your timing and consistency is accurate, you will work your way to not needing them.

Consider wearing small "English" style spurs until you have a feel for using spurs and are sure you aren't accidentally poking your horse. If you have short legs, it's sometimes more helpful to move to a longer spur once you have the feel for them—you can roll your leg and have contact without having to move your leg position.

And that is the best way to use spurs—ask your horse to move forward by bumping slightly with the sides of your calves. If you get no response, roll your foot out and roll your spur in—and move it out immediately! Your horse should move pretty quickly off the spur unless someone has gotten him dull to them.

You can use your spur to help move your horse's hindquarters either left or right as well.

Other Artificial Aids

The list is almost endless, but here are a few things you might also run across in your horse riding.

Tiedowns

The "tiedown" (called a "martingale" in English riding circles) is a strap that goes from the bridle to a breast collar on the saddle and simply prevents the horse from getting his head up beyond a certain point. Again, as with any artificial aid, the ideal is to teach your horse to keep his head at the level you want it without having to force him to do so (where's the horsemanship in that?). But if you have a horse that rears or seems always in danger of going over backward, the tiedown can be a way to prevent you from getting hurt. They are used quite a lot on kids' ponies.

Tiedowns/martingales can be "running" or "standing." The standing ones consist of one strap that holds the head down. "Running" means that there are two straps with rings that run through each of the reins. These have more give but they also put quite a lot of leverage on the bit.

What is the hackamore?
The hackamore bridle arrangement consists of three parts: the bosal, which is a round rawhide piece that goes around the nose; the hanger, which is a simple leather strap that holds the bosal on the horse's head; and a mecate (Spanish for "reins"), which in this case are long and attach around the base of the bosal. There is also a metal-laden "hackamore" that is commonly referred to as a "mechanical hackamore" and has no place in good horsemanship.

Nosebands

Nosebands are typically found on English bridles, not on Western ones. Although not usually thought of as an "artificial aid," nosebands that are cranked up tight are being used to hold the horse's mouth shut. Again, this is completely unnecessary if you just learn good horsemanship. Adjust the bit, try a new bit perhaps of a different metal, and learn to keep your hands quiet. Work with the horse's mental state and get him so he doesn't need to fuss with the bit when you are riding. Then you can use a noseband just because they look kind of classy, not because you need to tie your horse's mouth shut.

Anything Else!

In an attempt to get a horse to move, you can use almost anything you have at hand. In fact, if you are flexible and your arm is long enough, you can even slap your hand on the horse's rump. Western-style riders who use a mecate (looped reins long enough to create a sort of lead rope on the end) often use the tail end to give the horse a tap on the butt. If you ride with a lariat rope on your saddle, you can get some horses to go just by tapping the coils on the side of the saddle. Just be ready to ride whenever you try something new like that—you want "go" but you might get more than you bargained for!

Giving Up the Artificial Aids

Your goal with using artificial aids is to use them accurately enough to not need them anymore. Most Western riders wear spurs all the time, quite frankly, for style not purpose. The ranch cowboy wears spurs all the time: when doing ranch work if he needs to move fast, he doesn't want to be bargaining with his horse. So the spurs are always there if he needs them.

To be sure that you are working toward not needing these aids, there are two things to keep in mind.

Use the desired aid first. Always precede the artificial aid with the natural aid you want to be able to use. If you want your horse to go by bumping your legs, bump your legs, and if nothing happens follow up almost immediately with the crop or quirt. If you want to stop your horse by sitting heavier and deeper in the saddle, do that first before using the bit. If you are certain your horse will not respond to the aid you wish you could use, you can begin by doing them simultaneously—bump your legs and use the quirt. Once you feel him start to get the hang of what bumping your legs means, you can give him the benefit of the doubt first and use the quirt as follow up.

ALERT!

Think of artificial aids as just that—aids. Use them as a means to an end, not an end in themselves. Always work toward communicating with your horse by your natural aids. Whenever you pick up an artificial aid to use, think about how you can progress toward not using it. When first learning how to use a particular artificial aid or using one on a horse whose experience with that particular piece of equipment is not known, hold the aid so that you can simply drop it if your horse is afraid of it and things start to get out of hand.

You can pretty quickly make your horse dull to any aid, natural or artificial. Learn to be consistent and clear with your horse so you don't have to overdo use of the aids to the point that they hold no meaning for the horse.

Chapter 13

Balance, Timing, Feel, and Awareness

Almost everyone understands that to ride a horse, you need a certain amount of balance. To teach a horse, to ride a horse accurately, and to interact with him safely, you need to perfect your timing. And there is a third critical factor that has just started, in the past few years, to be explored more fully. This third factor is called "feel." But let's cover balance and timing first.

Balance

Prop yourself on a horse for the first time, and balance takes on a whole new meaning. There you are, several feet above the ground, on an animal that stretches several feet out in front of you and a couple of feet behind you. Your head—which represents a considerable amount of weight—is bobbing around way above the animal you are sitting on. And if all that isn't enough, add to the piece of the puzzle the fact that the horse is moving. Yikes! That will test anyone's balance.

In Chapter 5, you learned about some things you can do while on the ground to help increase your balance, like tai chi and yoga. At the end of this section, you'll find a couple of exercises you can do on horseback to help increase your balance.

FACT

Horses are programmed to be extremely aware. They are aware of their environment, what is immediate and what is on the horizon. They are aware of what you are doing at every moment that you are interacting with them, either while you are on the ground or on their backs. As humans, we can't match the awareness level of the horse, but we can learn a lot about awareness from them and use it to our advantage.

The most obvious reason that balance is important is that it helps you to not fall off your horse. That's always a good thing. But your ability to stay balanced is also very important to the horse. Balance adds to his comfort and his feeling of everything being okay despite that against all natural instincts he has allowed something to be strapped to his back and some living thing to cling to it.

When you are off balance on the horse's back, he will receive mixed messages from your aids. Your seat bones will be weighted differently, your legs and feet will work off-kilter. Extremely sensitive or young green horses often can't stand this feeling of your being off center on their backs. A rider who gets off balance can set this kind of horse to bucking, which is a key reason why inexperienced riders are not a good match for young horses (although there are always exceptions to this!).

Another problem with being off balance is that you will throw your saddle off balance. This means that the weight of your body and the pressure points of the saddle will be tilted to one side. This is not only disconcerting to the horse, but uncomfortable as well. And a critical factor here is that if your saddle is off balance, all the horse has to do is jump to one side at something and your saddle will end up on his side, which usually puts you on the ground. This can also send a horse into a bucking fit, since having a saddle strapped to his side is not something most horses are accustomed to. Some horses can hold it together pretty well under this kind of circumstance, others can't—it depends on the horse's general personality, the situation, how you react, and the horse's level of training.

ALERT!

Because horses are handled almost exclusively from the left side, they get quite adept at pushing on people from that side. This is where the horse sees a person most of the time, and the horse knows that he could make the person move if he moves into her space. When you begin to work with a horse from the right side, he might start off less able to operate smoothly when being led, for instance, but he also won't be accustomed to pushing in on that side!

Balance Exercises

One of the most common series of lesson exercises that instructors have students do are 1) ride without stirrups, 2) ride without reins, and 3) ride with your eyes closed. To do this, you need a solid trusty old school horse. Your instructor will put the horse on the end of a longe line so you don't have to worry about controlling the horse. The idea is to feel the horse's movements and to increase your balance astride the horse.

Riding Without Stirrups

Giving up your stirrups is a bit like giving up a security blanket. The stirrups help keep your legs in position on the sides of the horse. But beginning riders can get very dependent on the stirrups to achieve balance. And many times that works against the rider—when you push your feet too hard into the stirrup you also push yourself out of the saddle. During general riding, you want to use the stirrups as foot rests and use your seat and your upper leg to help balance you on the horse.

At faster gaits, your instructor will tell you time and time again to put your "heels down." Your heels become shock absorbers for the movement of your body because of the movement of the horse. But one exercise instructors ask riders to do without stirrups is to post, as we learned in the chapter on trotting. And you know what, you can.

If you get off balance without your stirrups, you'll know it pretty quickly. The idea of sliding out of the saddle is a good motivator for working on your balance. Of course, a good instructor who is focused on safety won't let the situation deteriorate to your sliding off the horse. These exercises need to be done gradually allowing you to slowly build up your balance and taking your riding to the next level.

Riding Without Reins

Beginning riders can be heavy-handed when it comes to how they hang onto the reins. One of the least desirable results of this is that they often use the horse's mouth for balance. Ouch! Hanging on tightly to the reins for balance will quickly dull your horse to the bit. And since the bit and reins are a major source of communication between rider and horse, it's important to avoid this. Riding without reins will encourage you to balance in your seat and your body and not use the horse's mouth for balance. A side benefit is that it can be a great tool for teaching you to use your leg aids better to direct the horse and not rely entirely on the bit.

Riding with Your Eyes Closed

This might sound scary, but it's actually great fun. You need to have complete trust in your horse and the person leading him. (NEVER do this on your own no matter how confident you are in your horse!) Spend the first few minutes with your eyes closed just getting comfortable with the whole idea. Then start to concentrate on how the horse is moving. His movements will become much more pronounced to you with your eyes closed. Have your handler turn corners, back the horse up, and go in circles so you can feel the full gamut of the horse's movements.

Also have the person leading the horse spend some time with the movement of each leg. For instance, she can tell you when the horse's right hind leg is just lifting off the ground. With your eyes closed, you can really concentrate on what movement you feel as the ground person tells you the leg is moving. In this case, you will feel the right hip pushing your seat up as the horse lifts its hind leg. Do this with all four legs, feeling the hip and shoulder movements required for the horse to move.

FACT

Because of the position of the horse's eyes on his head, he has two worlds to consider—the world that's out of his left eye, and a different one out of his right eye. They do have a certain range of "binocular" vision, but a large part of their vision is monocular. It's also important to know that horses have a blind spot immediately ahead of the nose and immediately behind the tail.

The Horse's Balance

Another interesting consideration when it comes to balance is paying attention to your horse being balanced. Somewhere in the dark ages, quite literally, it was determined that everything should be done from the left side of the horse—saddling, leading, mounting, bridling, and other tasks. Because of this, horses become very unbalanced.

If you have been riding for a while, you'll have also most likely done everything from the left. Try to bridle a horse from the right. Not only are you awkward, but your horse won't help you be less awkward since he's not accustomed to being dealt with from that side. But if you start using both sides of the horse when you are a beginner—for example, haltering him from both the left and right, leading him on the right and the left—you won't fall into the habit of just doing things from the left. Unfortunately, while this technique can really work when the horse is a beginner, the beginner rider/beginner horse setup isn't, as we've learned, the best match.

This also can be a little hard because most horse equipment is set up to be operated from the left side. Buckles on a bridle buckle on the left; the girths of the saddle do up on the left. English saddles can be a little easier to do things from the right; Western saddles either require you to reorganize the rigging or to make a few extra steps around the horse. Although if you become accustomed to putting your Western saddle on from the horse's right side, you will be already in the right spot to undo the cinches, and then you can step to the left and finish doing everything up. That way you get some convenience, and you both are using both sides.

E ALERT!

When you approach a horse that is new to you or is somewhat timid, extend your hand while moving toward him. A scratch on the shoulder or a rub on the neck is a nice sign that you are a worthy companion. When horses interact with each other, they never do anything that resembles the flat-palmed slap that a lot of people use to "pat" horses. Rub horses, don't slap them!

Pick a good old reliable, well-trained horse and try saddling him on the right. First get adept at smoothly putting the saddle blanket on and off. You'll get him used to that as well. If he doesn't stand for the saddle pad on the right, he's not going to stand for the saddle either so it might be best to find a different horse to try this with. Use as lightweight a saddle as you can find (e.g., an English saddle, even if you normally ride Western) since your arm muscles on that side won't be as developed as the ones on the side you lift your saddle up with typically. Lift the saddle on and off the horse. Work up to your typical saddle gradually.

Do this with everything—bridling, leading, administering paste deworming medication. Balance yourself and your horse!

Timing

Perfecting your timing is at once one of the most critical and most difficult things for beginning riders to accomplish. To time your reaction or action, you have to know what you are feeling for. One of the best ways to explain timing is in relation to the concept of "discipline" or "punishment" when it comes to horses.

Timing as Discipline

Horses live in an immediate world. If they touch an electric fence they get an immediate shock. This is why electric fences work so well—they have perfect timing! The horse can easily associate the shock with touching the fence. If the horse touched the fence and five seconds later got a shock, he might associate the shock with something else other than touching the fence. A delayed electric shock will most likely not work as well to contain the horse. This holds true for most of what the horse world thinks of as "punishment." It's just not quick enough to be fully effective.

ESSENTIAL

"Whether we're speeding the horse up, slowing him down, stopping, or backing him, we're working for a feel between rider and horse—less physical and more mental contact all the time." —Ray Hunt, from *Think Harmony with Horses*

You have your horse on a lead rope and are getting him ready to ride. He likes to bite at you when you go to tighten up the cinch. Many people think the solution to biting is to hit the horse when he bites. But by the time you hit him, he has already bitten you! He doesn't really associate the hit with the biting—at least not effectively enough for him to not bite again. He will continue to try to bite you, he might just pull his head back faster when he does to avoid the coming smack!

The horse needs to get a more immediately timed reaction to his bite. A better-timed reaction is to stick your elbow out and have the horse run into the hard end of your elbow (or hold the end of a crop to stick out from your elbow) when he swings his head to take a bite. This is immediate. It also has the added advantage of not being a reaction from you—the horse seems to think, in a case like this, that he inflicted the pain onto himself by the very act of attempting to bite.

Timing Your Aids for the Request

When you ask a horse to move in a certain way with your aids—natural or artificial—you need to time them as closely as possible. The key to timing your aids is to ask the horse to do something when the horse is in the position to actually do what you are requesting.

To do something as simple as moving the horse's right front foot back while he is at a standstill, it is most important to know where the horse's weight is. If he is standing with his weight on that right front foot, he cannot move it without first shifting his weight. So when you request that foot to move, you need to consider that the horse might need to first shift his weight from that right front foot onto the left one to pick that foot up off the ground.

This also holds true for more complicated moves like flying lead changes (where the horse changes his leading foot midstride, see Chapter 10 for details). To change leads, the horse has to move his shoulder over to give him the freedom he needs to use that side as his leading foot.

Timing for the Release

Horses are always looking for the spot where there is no pressure. When pressure is applied to them, they learn at the point of release of the pressure. So if you pick up on the reins and put pressure on his mouth, whatever he is doing when you release that pressure is what he thinks you wanted him to do. And he will do it again. If you release him when he feels several pounds of weight in your hands, you will be teaching him that you want several pounds of weight in your hands when you pick up on the reins (you do not!). This is the classic place where you need to "be careful what you ask for."

This could happen for every direction you give the horse. For instance, you are standing in the aisle and someone wants to get by you on the left.

You want your horse to step to his right so you both can get out of the way. You put your hand on his left shoulder and press in to him to request him to move away from the pressure. Instead he moves in to the pressure and pushes into your hand. But the person going by slipped by anyway, so you removed your hand even though the horse never stepped to the right and *even though he is still pushing into your hand.* That release of pressure at the moment told the horse that pushing against you was the right thing to do. By doing that, he got relieved from the pressure of your hand pushing into him.

If you do this, it's certainly not the end of the world! It doesn't mean your horse can now never learn that when you press your hand against him, you want him to step away from it, move his head away, or some other movement. However, it does make the job of teaching him what you want a bit more difficult. Depending on the horse, he could quickly unlearn the incorrect direction and learn what you really meant. Or he might take quite a few lessons to get the right idea. On your part, it is critical to be *aware* of what took place instead of ignoring it. In fact, set up opportunities to work this lesson in and teach the horse what you really meant.

ALERT!

If a horse is prone to nipping, nibbling, or biting people, the first thing to do is to stay away from his mouth as much as possible. Do not hand feed him (this is often a reason the horse starts biting) and do not rub his muzzle. This is especially important with young horses. They tend to be curious and tactile with their mouths, so it's best not to set them up to bite you. Young horses bite each other, and they are unaware that it hurts you more than their corral mate!

The Concept of "Feel"

Horses operate on what is called "feel." Feel is a difficult concept to describe. It's almost a sixth sense—or at least a highly refined extension of the sense of touch. When it comes to working with horses, feel isn't just the physical tactile experience you have with your horse. This just skims the surface of the meaning. Although it isn't a mystical thing either—you don't have to place rocks in certain circle patterns or wear specific receptive clothing or anything like that. It really requires just you and the horse. Learning how to "feel of a horse" allows you to understand and sense when you are doing just enough.

Most animals are highly sensitive. Horses are no exception. They are hyperaware mentally as well as physically, having been programmed to be on the lookout for danger of any kind. The horse's main goal in life seems to be to simply want to get along so that he doesn't have to live in a state of concern.

It's this sensitivity that horseback riders can use to their advantage if they are willing to learn certain techniques. The wonderful and unique thing about riding horses is that, unlike a motorcycle, car, or bicycle, the horse has a mind. He is thinking about what is happening at this very moment every moment of the day. In return for the horse allowing us to use him as a source of entertainment, the least we can do is to allow him to use his mind and to consider what his thoughts might be in any given situation.

FACT

If you have ever driven a standard-shift car, you know lots about timing and feel. To coordinate the release of the clutch with acceleration and shift with smoothness, you need to time these two things. You need to gain a feel for when the clutch is about to engage and feel just how much pressure you should put on the gas pedal to make a smooth transition.

A horse that moves forward when the slack is just about to come out of the lead rope is operating on feel. A horse that has to have the lead rope tugged on to make him move is not. The same horse that has to be dragged when a human tries to lead him will probably move away from another horse above him in the pecking order of the herd without the lead horse having to even touch him. Just the pressure of the intensity of the lead horse's gaze or movement is enough to move the first horse. The horse, in that situation, is operating on feel. Feel is the language of the horse.

Learning about how to feel of a horse will give you a much better riding experience. It takes some experience with working horses to gain a sense of feel. Don't give up just because you seem so clumsy and awkward around horses at first. Everyone is clumsy and awkward while learning anything! Horses seem to understand intention, and most will reward it with a good try. Even the person with no feel at all, someone who slaps horses to show affection, who is gruff and loud and yanks the reins around often has some level of success with horses if his intentions are good.

Awareness

Awareness could be a fourth critical component to working with horses but it really is more a critical aspect of each of the three components—balance, timing, and feel—presented here. If you just mindlessly stumble around horses, you will not only jeopardize your safety but on a subtler level, you will never develop your balance, timing, and feel to the level of being extremely and satisfyingly effective with horses.

Awareness comes in at every level of working with the horse. When you are leading the horse, do you know that he is paying no attention to you and is about to dive for grass and drag you with him? When you are putting the bridle on, are you poking the opposite side of the headstall into the horse's eye? When you swing on the saddle, are you careful that you tied up the off-side cinches so that the buckle of the cinch doesn't swing down and bang him on his right elbow?

Horses are at once huge and powerful and also enormously sensitive. They seem extremely appreciative of people who are aware and who have perfected their balance, timing, and feel. This is obvious by how quickly they respond to someone who has these attributes in good measure. Horsemen and horsewomen who have perfected their horsemanship to this degree can accomplish amazing things with horses in a relatively short amount of time.

Magical But Not Magic

When you've perfected your timing and awareness, you'll sense when the horse is just about to do what you are asking. Then you'll stop asking at that point, and your horse will start to pick up what you want very quickly. This all builds to a mutual feeling that begins to look like your horse can read your mind. The horse kind of can read your mind. But what he is really reading is that when you have a thought—back up, turn left—you'll subconsciously begin to shift your body in subtle ways. And the horse can feel that subtleness. That is what a horse is designed to do physically, physiologically, and mentally. It's not magic, but it can be the most magical feeling to really get in tune with your horse.

QUESTION?

I'm trying to be a more effective rider and handler, but it's a lot to consider all at once! What is most important—balance, timing, or feel?

Feel is probably the most important of the three. But it seems impossible to have feel without the other two. By perfecting your balance, you can perfect your timing. By perfecting your timing, you can perfect your feel. And by increasing your awareness around horses, all three can come a little faster. Who said good horseback riding was easy?

Chapter 14

Arena Work

There are two main locations where the casual rider rides horses. One is on the trail; the other is in the arena. The arena probably outweighs the other in terms of how much time you will spend, especially if you are taking lessons. A beginning rider could be timid on the trail and should be cautious on trail rides until she becomes comfortable on a horse. And for anyone looking to go into the show ring, riding in the arena environment is often where most of the learning—for both the rider and the horse—goes on.

Inside or Out?

A large boarding facility in almost any part of the country will have both an indoor and an outdoor arena. Neither is inherently better; there are advantages and disadvantages to both.

The Indoor Arena

In northern climates, indoor riding arenas provide riders with a place to ride in the winter. In most instances, this isn't necessary because of temperature, however; it's because of footing. Although your farrier can put winter shoes on your horse (shoes similar to the usual ones except the shoes have cleats that grip the ice) many times the footing is just too slippery to be safe. And even when the footing is reasonably safe for a walk through the woods, if you want to do any kind of faster paced schooling, you need access to an indoor arena.

FACT

While the idea of a "bombproof" horse is nice, every horse has something that will set him off. You should always have done lots of "sacking out" exercises—helping him work through loud sounds like a plastic bag blowing in the wind, a flapping tarp, or a rain slicker shaking around him. Although he has a right to be scared at whatever scares him, the horse that is truly safe to ride learns how to hold himself together with your support.

Typically, an indoor arena won't provide much relief from the cold. In fact, some of them might feel colder than the weather outside since they trap cold air like a refrigerator. But the trend with newer arenas, especially in the extreme northern climates like the Upper Midwest, is to have heaters installed. These heaters don't actually "heat" the arena—in fact, you don't really want your horse with his long winter coat to have to work in an arena that is too warm—but they do take the bite out of the intense cold that these cavernous buildings can trap. Sometimes simply being insulated can help ward off the severe cold in an indoor arena, but again, the insulation can also serve as a trap for cold air.

Before you sign on to board at a specific facility, talk to a couple of people who have ridden in the indoor arena, especially in the wintertime, and get a sense of how comfortable they find the temperature. But remember, everyone is different in her tolerance for cold and her preferences for other amenities.

In warmer climates, the indoor arena provides some relief from heat. In all climates, the indoor arena could be a welcome relief for you and your horse to have a place to ride where you aren't fighting the bugs of summer. And in all climates, whether it's raining or snowing, and you just want to putter around without getting soaked, the indoor arena provides shelter from precipitation.

Most indoor arenas are wood or metal buildings. However, in the past decade or so, a new kind of fabric-covered arena has become increasingly popular. There are a couple of significant advantages to these kinds of arenas. Although they are sturdy, significant buildings, most towns consider them temporary structures. so that they do not have the tax implications of typically constructed indoor arenas. And they are incredibly light inside since the fabric is translucent. Even on a dreary winter afternoon, the fabric covered arena at least captures what light there is available.

You will want to accustom your horse to the indoor arena environment before you get on and just gallop around. If it's excessively windy out, it can sound pretty ominous in the hollow space of an indoor arena. While being ridden in the arena, the horse could hear someone walking a horse around the outside or other noises outside that the horse can't see, and this could be disconcerting to him. Not just rain and sleet, but even the sound of bird feet scratching on the roof can be magnified to a terrifying noise. And the sound of snow sliding off an arena roof can be deafening; although you can't do much to train your horse ahead of time to deal with that, you can do other "bombproofing" training (see sidebar) to prepare him for the occasional loud scary noise.

Indoor arenas increase the amount of board a facility can (and must) charge. If you don't think you will ride very often in the winter months, it's probably not worth it to pay the extra it would cost to board at a facility with an indoor arena. However, if access to an indoor arena is important to you, plan ahead, since openings at these facilities get filled up pretty fast as the winter approaches.

Outdoor Arenas

Outdoor arenas often seem larger than indoor ones, even when they are the same size. The enclosed space of an indoor arena gives it a feeling of being smaller and more closed-in. The horse surely feels that way too! An outdoor arena (commonly referred to as a "ring"), even if it isn't significantly larger physically, will still feel larger, and, of course, more open.

Outdoor arenas can be made any size that the area can accommodate, without the cost or materials needed to build a large enclosed indoor arena. There are fewer costs associated with the outdoor arena, which could mean the facility without an indoor arena is cheaper for you. However, the cost of appropriate footing in an arena, indoor or outdoor, runs into thousands of dollars, so keep that in mind if you think of creating one at home.

Photograph by Bob Atkins

▲ Using an outdoor arena.

Most boarding barns also give lessons. Find out what the lesson schedule is. If the arena is big enough, you can probably ride while one individual is having a private lesson. But if there is a group lesson going on or the arena is small, you not only won't want to be riding at the same time, you might not be able to.

Safety

There are many things about arenas, both indoor and out, which you will want to consider when it comes to safety. If you are shopping for a boarding or riding facility with an indoor arena, be wary of it being used for storage as well as riding. You don't want to ride around a tractor in the corner, a stack of metal fencing against the side. If things are stored in the arena, they should be fenced off in a corner and out of the way.

Equipment should not be hanging off the sides of the walls so that you might get your foot caught as you ride by.

Perhaps most important with the outdoor arena, do not make a temporary arena out of things like metal fence posts. If you fall off your horse, you often don't have a choice of where you land and landing on one of those posts could be lethal. Wood posts with wood fencing is still the safest way to surround an outdoor arena.

Lighting for indoor arenas is usually very carefully thought out. Most indoor arenas have some translucent panels along the sides and several large sliding doors that can be opened to let in light in the daytime. But what about riding in the evenings? You will want to know where the light switches are and whether it's okay to come in the evenings and turn on the lights to ride.

People often forget about lighting for outdoor arenas. Of course, being outside, you usually have all the light you need during the day during the summer. But the useable time of an outdoor arena can be extended greatly by having lights available, especially in the winter time when the dark hours exceed daylight hours. In the western part of the country, there are more public arenas; like tennis courts and other kinds of outdoor activities, some places put in light switches that turn on when you put in money. If you are already paying top dollar for board, lights should be included. But paying for lighting this way might tempt a facility without outdoor lighting to install it.

Arena Etiquette

As with anything we do where we have to interact with others, there are some etiquette issues specific to arenas.

When you enter the indoor arena with your horse, alert riders inside that you are coming (some establishments have you yell "door" or whatever—you should get a tour and instructions on what the key word is). They need to know that a door is going to open in on them as they are riding around. And they need to be able to be prepared in case their horse pays more attention to the incoming horse than his rider.

It's probably best for everyone to ride in the same direction. If there is just you and one other person riding, it won't matter as much, there's plenty of room for you to get out of each other's way.

When passing someone in the same direction, you should go to the inside and should call ahead that you are passing. When passing each other while riding in opposite directions, pass with the person going counterclockwise on the rail. That said, always check the facility for its specific rules.

Don't expect to mix jumping with casual riding in the indoor arena with several people there. This is where it can be critical to pick a facility with a riding focus similar to what you are interested in doing with your horse.

In a small, casual boarding facility where there are never more than two or three riders in the arena at a time, you can probably avoid a lot of fussy etiquette issues. But in an active facility with many people riding at once, etiquette is as much for safety as for politeness! There might be other etiquette issues and rules specific to the facility you decide to board at. Be sure to check.

Arena Size

Arenas are usually a minimum of 70 feet wide and 100 feet long, although they really could be of almost any size. Most indoor arenas will be large enough to accommodate a few riders. The cost of building an arena is quite large and a facility that has one usually needs to be able to take in a few boarders to help pay for it. But if you are building an arena or buying a place with one already built (either indoor or outdoor), almost any size from

60 feet wide and 80 feet long or larger can work. The narrower the arena, the quicker the horse needs to turn corners. And the longer the long stretch, the more the horse gets a chance to move out.

If you are checking out arenas to find a place to board your horse or lease a horse, ask if the arena is used for loose turnout. Most people have a limited time to ride so you probably don't want to spend a portion of your time at the barn rounding up loose horses so you can use the arena.

Different Kinds of Arenas

Different disciplines require different types of arenas. For instance, to prepare for a dressage competition, you need to be at an arena where the ring is of the proper size and has letters placed in the appropriate spots for your level of competition. To work on a reining pattern, you need an arena with plenty of space and footing conducive to the sliding required in stops. We'll review some of the arena traits needed from simple to more complex.

Pleasure Riding

Whether you are simply trying to keep your horse fit over the winter while awaiting trail riding season or you like to compete in the pleasure horse show circuit, pleasure riding is going to require the least complicated arena. A lot of what you will do is ride around in circles in both directions. However, be sure to read the section at the end of this chapter on how not to bore your horse. Even if you are focused on pleasure riding, you are smart to add some interest to the ride besides circles.

Trail

If actual trail riding or trail classes in the show ring are your thing, it can be great fun coming up with ideas for "obstacles" in the arena environment. Obstacles don't have to be complicated. An obstacle only has to require some of the moves that your horse will need to accomplish while on the trail or in the trail class. If the gate is not in a place that is easy to work on opening from horseback, you can build a simple gate to place in the arena. Just be sure it's easy to move. If building a moveable gate seems like too much work, you can set up ground rails in a pattern that require the same moves you would need to get up to and through a gate. You can set up a mailbox (also moveable!) or put a tarp down to walk over or put cross rails down with bushes on each side. The ideas are only limited by your imagination.

ALERT!

Whenever you set up jumps or crossrails with live bushes on the sides, be sure that the bushes are not toxic to horses! Many decorative landscaping shrubs and trees are poisonous to livestock. Just a couple of mouthfuls snatched from a yew bush, for example, as a horse goes by could be enough to make him seriously ill, even to the point of death. If you are not sure, don't use the landscaping shrubs, it's just not worth it.

Barrel Racing and Pole Bending

To practice barrel racing and pole bending and other gymkhana games, you will need quite a lot of space. The amount of space taken up by the barrels or poles isn't a lot, but you need to be able to run in to the course and run out. You might not be able to set up the standard distances but don't expect your horse to cut sharp corners at a full gallop! This is the kind of instance where you would do best to find a facility that caters to the type of activity you want to do. The appropriate facility will probably have a permanent barrel course set up.

Reining

As mentioned earlier, reining patterns are usually performed in competition in a huge stadium. You can still practice bits and pieces in a smaller arena but don't expect long slides in the sliding stop if the arena isn't very long or the footing is like glue under the horse's feet. Reining is a rather unique riding discipline (and it's also being considered for an Olympic sport!). In this discipline, you would do best to find a facility that focuses on reining.

Cow Work

Working with cows, such as training for cutting competitions or team penning, has some special requirements when it comes to the arena. First, there needs to be a holding pen (preferably with shade and access to water) where the rest of the cows can hang out when you are using just a couple of them. The other is that the fencing needs to be adequate enough to hold a cow who desperately wants out. That not only means the fence needs to be strong, but it needs to have fence boards spaced close enough together so that a cow can't slip between the boards.

Jumping

Jumping requires some space to spread jumps at appropriate distances. But one of the key factors that must be considered when building an arena in which jumping is a prime activity is head room! You don't want low rafters when your horse is sailing over 4' jumps. And the same as any equine discipline that requires ground equipment, it's great when you can be at a facility where the jumps can be left in place.

Dressage

Dressage arenas have very specific measurement requirements. Large dressage arenas (used mainly in upper levels of competition) are 60 meters long by 20 meters wide (approximately 197 feet by 66 feet). Small dressage arenas are 40 meters long by 20 meters wide (approximately 132 feet by 66 feet). Letters are spaced around the perimeter—the larger arena has five letters evenly spaced down the long sides and through the middle; smaller arenas have three letters down the sides, with only 6 meters from either end, and 14 meters between the middle letters. You can buy ready-made dressage letters or you can make them yourself. If your dressage arena consists of a chalk line or ground poles (i.e., you don't have a wall to stick the letters on), you can buy letters on stakes, or you can make them out of milk cartons with sand in them. Get creative, it can be fun! The point is, it's important that the arena has the dimensions of your level of competition since you will want to be able to practice in an accurately sized space.

Keep the Horse Interested

Riding arenas can lead to a lot of mindless riding in boring circles. While it's good to warm you and your horse up with some walk, trot, canter circles around an arena, after fifteen or twenty minutes you and your horse will get bored. Even if you don't plan to do any of the obstacle-driven disciplines, using some obstacles or props can help keep arena work interesting for both you and your horse.

Ground Poles

A simple way to add some interest to arena riding is with ground poles. Ground poles are poles around 10' long and 4" in diameter. You can use logs, the rails from post-and-rail fencing, or even PVC plumbing pipe. It helps if the poles are round since they will easily roll if the horse hits one.

If you want to create some visual aid, paint your ground poles different colors and run a foot-wide white stripe around the middle or paint them in stripes so that there are two white and three colored, allowing for a middle stripe. That way you can set yourself patterns like cross over the yellow pole at the middle stripe, sidepass down the red pole, back between the two green poles, and cross back over the yellow pole at the right stripe, etc.

Some simple exercises to do with ground poles are:

- Lay two poles approximately 3 feet apart and walk between them straight and down the middle.
- Back through the same two ground poles.
- Add two more poles perpendicular to each of the first two. Walk to the corner, turn your horse on the forehand, and walk out. Do this again, only turn the hindquarters around the front to turn the corner. Be sure to leave yourself enough room for whichever end you are using to turn.
- Back through the corner configuration you set up above.

- Set three or four ground poles approximately 4 feet apart and trot through them.
- If you have enough poles, set up all the above and create a fun course to work through!

FACT

Poles that are attached on either end to supports in the shape of an X are called "cavelettis." These are great training tools for horses. The X supports are created so that when you prop them on one end, they are a few inches off the ground, and when you prop them on the other end, they are a few more inches off the ground.

Barrels

Even if barrel racing doesn't interest you, you can use barrels similar to how you use ground poles to create some interest in the arena environment. Some horses might need to just get used to the barrels standing there! If you use the big plastic water drums, be careful not to get too close when you are first familiarizing your horse with barrels. These drums could easily be knocked over and scare a horse simply by falling. The situation could be much worse if the barrel gets underneath the horse's body! Set barrels in patterns, and use them to help you be more accurate in your riding.

Always keep safety at the top of your list of priorities. Don't use poles that could harm your horse. For example, a pole only 3 feet long with a pointed end could impale the horse if he stepped on one end and a point stuck into him. PVC can be slippery, so keep that in mind if your horse steps on top of one. And it's best to never let a horse loose in an arena with props set up.

Chapter 15
Trail Riding

Probably the most common kind of riding that the casual rider will do outside the lesson ring is trail riding. This is what many people think of when they picture horseback riding—a leisurely stroll through the woods on the back of a beautiful horse. Riding a safe horse on safe yet challenging trails is perhaps the most fun a human being can have.

Why Trail Ride?

Moseying horseback through the woods, across the beach, around the edge of a green pasture, or across the prairie is a peaceful and great way to enjoy the outdoors. For most people who want to ride horses, this is what they think of when they imagine themselves on horseback.

But there's more to it than just riding off into the sunset. Your horse needs to be prepared for what he might see out on the trail. And you need to know how to deal with diversions that might come up. Nothing at all might come up on many rides, but if you ride enough, odds are that an animal will run across the trail or a bird will squawk loudly nearby. It's best to know how to calm your horse before this happens.

Riders who compete in ring-oriented competitions like horse shows, dressage competitions, and even show jumping would do well to get their horses out on the trails once in a while. Don't fall into the trap of getting so focused on the show ring that your horse will completely freak out if you ask him to move somewhere without a rail beside him. Some show horses simply cannot take trail riding—the setting that they see most of the time is so artificial that the real world is too much for them. And they become so accustomed to the level even footing of the show ring that they don't know how to move smoothly when the ground is uneven and rocky. But if you get out on the trails early in the horse's show career, you can help him immensely. And simply seeing something different will help him from getting sour and bored. Trail riding can help any horse both mentally and physically.

Maneuvers on the Trail

You don't have to restrict "schooling" to the ring. A ride out into the countryside can include plenty of so-called schooling. Moving around trees and in tight spaces that come up on the trail can reinforce ring work you've done to help him learn to move off your leg. There's no rule that says you have to aim your horse straight down the trail; you can weave him slightly left, then right, then left, and help him soften in the bit and work off your leg. You can introduce him or reinforce the idea of sidepassing, where he moves "laterally"—first both his left legs move over, then both his right. All this helps get your horse better at yielding. You can trot down the trail and practice half halts (pulling slightly on one rein to help break his forward momentum just a hair at a time). And trail riding with some friends gives your horse opportunities to get accustomed to being around other horses in different settings. All these things help create the well-rounded, well-schooled horse.

The Mental Aspect

Sometimes trail riding for the horse in competition can simply give the horse a chance to relax and see something different. If you are afraid that your horse's slow Western jog will be ruined by letting him trot out when he's out on the trail, then perhaps you can begin and end the show season with some trail riding. But once you improve your horsemanship skills enough, you won't let these fears get in your way. Give your horse—and you!—a mental break, you'll both do better for it.

Local Trails

If you board your horse, lease a horse at a boarding facility, or if you just take lessons, you will have the advantage of being in a place where someone has probably already figured out all the local trails. In fact, many riding facilities have a couple of miles of trails accessible right from the facility. Otherwise, find out if there is a trail riding club in your area—not only will the club's members know about good trails that are open to horses, but clubs often sponsor trail rides during the year. Snowmobile clubs can also be good ways to find trails; see if they create a map that they distribute to club members. Using snowmobile trails can be the only way to ride in some snowy climates, but usually the good thing about these trails is that you are typically using them at a time of year when the snowmobiles are not.

ALERT!

If you are a cigarette smoker, never smoke while trail riding. It takes very little to start a forest fire. Cigarettes and trails don't mix.

If you have a trailer or a friend you ride with has one, you can venture a little farther afield. Some state parks have horse riding trails. A few states have worked on taking old railroad beds and turning them into multiuse trails. In Chapter 19 you will find some great places around the country to ride, like the Gettysburg battlefields in Pennsylvania or Acadia National Park in Maine.

Never ride on trails without getting permission first. Even if the local snowmobile club has permission to ride on someone's land, horseback riders should get their own permission. Some landowner's allow snowmobiles to use their land because by design snowmobiles never touch the ground; they need snow to move on, so their impact can be lower than other trail users. And you don't want to jeopardize the snowmobile club's access by abusing its privileges.

Ask around about ownership of areas you are interested in riding on. If no one knows or you suspect their assumption might be wrong, check the town's tax maps to find out who owns the land. Be prepared to exchange some work in return for riding privileges. Trail clearing/trimming twice yearly or your helping mow a seeded road can be of benefit to the landowner.

Trail Riding Preparation

There are some things about riding on trails that you can't simulate—a deer suddenly running across the trail or a pheasant being flushed from the brush—but there are lots of things that you can. First, and most important, be sure the horse you plan to trail ride knows the fundamentals of being ridden—he should be yielding and soft in your hands, and he should be able to move each of his feet at your direction. Most important, you should have developed a good rapport to provide him with the confidence and support he needs so he doesn't feel like he has to take over, putting both of you in danger. The foundation for all this can all be accomplished in the confines of a riding ring; once you get out on the trails, you will want to further build on these fundamentals.

Once you have some good horsemanship going, you can set up some obstacles for your horse to maneuver. Ground poles to cross and barrels to go around can mimic logs and trees. Work with him on crossing tarps. Make a "flag" by putting a bandana or even a plastic shopping bag on the end of a crop or stiff stick and expose him to something flapping around him. Get out your rain slicker and expose him to that. Make use of that big puddle from yesterday's rain storm and show your horse he can get his feet wet and survive. Have a friend ride a mountain bike around in the arena with him where you can keep the situation calm and controlled.

FACT

Learn the signs that a horse makes before he kicks—ears back, shifting weight, and swinging his rear end are just a few of these warning signs. A horse can't kick while he is moving forward, so if your horse has shown a tendency to want to kick when he feels confined by other riders, keep your horse moving out. Sometimes when a horse is tapped with a crop, the end of the reins, or with your spurs, he might kick out before moving out. Be aware of where other riders are so you don't get them accidentally kicked.

Even though your horse might still get concerned when he sees the very same things out in the environment of the trail, all the exposure you can provide him with beforehand will give him more of a chance of holding it together.

Photographs by Bob Atkins

◀ Prepare your horse for trail riding by introducing obstacles.

▶ Using props can help you become more accurate and keep your horse more interested.

Photographs by Bob Atkins

Fitness for the Horse

The trail horse must be kept at a good level of fitness for the kind of riding you expect of him. If you can't ride your horse much during the week but want to take him on long trail rides over the weekend, you should find someone who can ride your horse during the week to help you keep him fit. It's only fair to the horse. And you should probably plan to make a couple of visits to the gym during the week yourself, if you want to be comfortable with your weekend warrior routine. Although there isn't much that can exactly simulate horseback riding, just keeping in shape can help a lot.

Build up your horse gradually at the beginning of the riding season. Work on muscle tone and wind capacity. After the first initial rides, begin to do a lot of trotting with short canters to break up the monotony, alternating with walks so that the horse can regain his breath. Changing gaits a lot can help build muscle tone, especially in the horse's back. Finding some trails with good footing that go up hills is a good way to build his lung capacity.

Always cool down your horse after a workout. If he sweats a lot, and the temperatures are favorable, hose him down. If the air is cool, use a lightweight blanket known as a "cooler," to cool him out and dry the sweat. If he drinks along the trail that is best. Otherwise, allow him to drink when he gets back but don't let him guzzle a couple of buckets all at once. Offer him water every ten minutes or so and let him cool off slowly.

E ALERT!

Bring your cell phone along, but don't rely on it to help you in an emergency. Cell phones often do not have reception in trail riding areas. And be sure your horse has a chance to hear your cell phone ring in a controlled situation—so he won't be startled by it—before you are out on the trail, and he hears it for the first time!

The Good Trail Horse

What makes a good trail horse? Confidence, calmness, and a willingness to go are three important traits. However, the horse doesn't have to be born with these traits, the rider can help instill them in the horse. And conversely, the rider who doesn't know how to encourage these traits could turn them off in a horse that had them either naturally or would have them with the help of another rider.

Confidence

A horse's confidence can be greatly impacted by his early riding experience. For the beginner rider, it's best to get a horse that has had some positive experience and that clearly possesses the self-confidence to be out on the trail. In fact, not only should the horse be confident, but he should have experienced a lot of different situations already so his exposure level is high. Some horses are naturally more confident than others. If you are buying a horse with the intention of riding on trails, you want to make sure the horse has a certain amount of boldness that makes him a good trail prospect.

ALERT!

Leave your ego at home when you go on a trail ride. Don't put yourself in danger just because you would be embarrassed to have to get off your horse, or you are frustrated that your horse won't do what you want. Sometimes getting off—when your horse is too wound up or he adamantly refuses to cross a bridge that looks dangerous to him—is simply the smarter thing to do.

Calmness

A high-strung horse is probably not the best match for a rider who just wants to ho-de-do along the trails. Trail riding involves a lot to take in. The experienced rider can support the more active horse on a busy trail ride, but the less experienced rider would do well to ride a horse that is either calm by nature or has enough trail experience to be calm because he has been well exposed to all the challenges.

Forward Movement

A horse you have to beg to move along is a tough horse to take out on the trails. Some horses are just lazy or slow by nature; others have become dull to the rider's legs. You can teach these horses to move out but that can be a tough project for a beginning rider. Pick a horse that is a willing mover so your legs don't get tired just from bumping him along all the time.

Trail Riding Vices

There are certain dangers and temptations your horse is exposed to when he's on the trail, so you must be prepared for these and know how to keep the horse—and you—safe.

Eating

Most horses will at least occasionally attempt to eat leaves along the side of the trail. If the horse you ride is so interested in eating he isn't paying attention to you, be sure to take care of this. Have an experienced person help you get your horse beyond this bad habit. An occasional snatch at leaves that are right in front of the horse's face is probably tough to avoid. However, some horses get so consumed by the idea of eating along the trail and they hang onto the branch so hard that they end up going in the wrong direction and practically catapult their rider off when the branch swings back. This is rude at best and dangerous at worst. And to add to the problem, there are many leaves that are poisonous to horses.

Kicking

Some horses have difficulty being too close to other horses on the trail. Sometimes a horse that never kicks out at another horse while trail riding might find a particular horse puts him on the defensive. Horses have to stop, if only for a second, to kick out. If you get in a crowded situation, try to keep your horse moving along to lessen the opportunity for him to kick at the horse behind him. Always plan ahead so that you keep your horse at least a couple of kick-lengths behind the next horse. Don't forget, a kick might injure your horse, and the kick could just as easily injure you.

Herd Bound

Many horses while on the trail get pretty hooked up with at least one of the other horses, maybe all. If one horse trots, the others trot without being requested to by the rider. If your riding companion gets out of sight, your horse might get pretty wound up about catching up. You need to shut this behavior down a notch or two before it becomes uncontrollable.

If your horse is prancing and trotting, don't try to force him to a walk, you will probably do nothing more than frustrate you both. Providing that, in your horse's training, he has been taught to yield to your aids, you can take a couple of actions:

- *Get him to slow down in stages.* Pick up on one rein and pull back a slight amount until you feel him yield—not just in his head but in his feet. Do this on both sides until you have slowed him down to a trot that is controlled by you and that you are comfortable with. Pulling back on both reins usually just sets up a fighting match and makes him go faster trying to escape all that pressure.

- *Use his excess energy until he burns up a bit of it and decides going slower or even walking is a whole lot less work.* Horses do not like to be mentally wound up, and they do not like to do more work than is necessary (those are big bodies to move around!). So if the trail is wide enough, you can let them release some of their energy by trotting them out yet doing serpentines along the trail. This serves the purpose not only of letting off some steam, but it can get the horse more focused on you by having to pay attention to what you are requesting. And you want the horse focused on you, and not the other horse that disappeared around the corner.

Racing

Many horses will take up racing when riding side by side with another horse. If your horse is this way, and you feel you must canter with your riding partner, be prepared to shut down your horse before he gets out of your control. The ability to do this starts back in the confines of the riding ring with your horse's fundamental education. Getting him willing to yield, to do half halts, to move his front quarters and his hind quarters at your request won't stop him from racing with other horses. These tools will help when the situation arises. Once the horse learns that if he races with the other horse, you will shut him down every time, he might start to think he ought to canter at your preferred pace and not his wild steeplechase mode.

Overexposure

There is a lot of value to exposing horses to different things, but *over-exposing* them can be detrimental to you both. When you are teaching your horse about scary objects such as tarps, rain slickers, grain sacks, and other items that could simulate things you might find on the trail, stop when things are good. You can always do it again the next day. If you drill and drill and drill on the same thing, you will blast right past the horse's acceptance of the thing and get him wound up again. How do you know when he's good about a certain thing? When you pick up the rain slicker the next day and he is right where he was when you put it down the day before, you probably can consider him sufficiently exposed. And a refresher once in a while never hurts.

QUESTION?

I've been shopping for a horse for myself for a few months now. I just want a horse I can get on and ride, but I can't seem to find one. Why not?
If you want something you can "just get on and ride" you should be shopping for a bicycle or a motorcycle, not a horse. Horses are animals with brains, which means they have thoughts and feelings. Your horsemanship goal is for the horse's thoughts to become the same as your thoughts. And a horse that interacts well with and respects one person is probably not going to automatically transfer that respect to you—you must earn it.

Trail Etiquette

When it comes to riding with others on the trail, there are a lot of things to consider.

- Once you are saddled up and ready to go, do not head off until everyone in your group is in the saddle and ready.
- If the trail is narrow, go single file and leave distance between you and the horse ahead of you. Try to let the horse with the fastest pace be out in front.
- When riding side by side on a wider trail, be aware of how the horses are interacting with each other so you can head off kicking or biting.
- Never just trot or canter off ahead without alerting your riding companions. Riders whose horses tend to take control could get into difficult situations this way. Let the other riders know what you are

going to do so they can have time to prepare for how their horses might react.

- Always alert someone if you are going to pass her and tell her which side you are passing on, especially on trails that aren't much wider than the width of two horses.

- Help each other get through obstacles on the trail. If there is an older, more experienced horse among the group, that horse could help the others with confidence in crossing water or bridges or any difficult obstacle.

- When you come across other riders on the trail, be courteous and help their group and yours stay calm and stay together.

The number one trail etiquette rule is to take out everything you take in. In some areas, you are even expected to clean up after your horse on the trail. At the very least, clean up any manure your horse produces while at the trailhead parking area as well as at rest stops, picnic areas, or anywhere that nonriders use, even if the best you can do is kick it off into the bushes. If you don't, someday you might return to ride and find "no horseback riding" signs posted.

Competing on the Trail

You can compete as a trail rider. There are several levels of competition each with its own twist on judging criteria. However, a common rule for them all is that your horse must not be completely spent at the end of the ride.

Judged Trail Rides

A simple judged trail ride is usually 10 to 15 miles. You and your horse are checked as you go out and checked when you come in. The trails chosen for a judged ride have some natural or created obstacles, and a judge at a couple of the obstacles will watch you and your horse navigate the stream or the bridge crossing. Although time is not a deciding factor in ribbon placing, there is usually an outside time limit (e.g., "all riders must be in by 1 P.M."). Depending on the size of the club or the number of riders, ribbons are awarded in different categories.

Competitive Trail Rides

Competitive trail rides are a bit more serious than the casual judged trail ride. These rides are also judged, but they are typically won on the more objective framework of time—the horse/rider team that comes in first wins. But there is always the rule that your horse must be in good condition at the end. Most competitive rides will take the horse's vital signs such as pulse and respiration before you leave and when you come in. A team whose horse is struggling will not win even with the best time.

ALERT!

When trail riding on multiuse trails, you will surely come across a snowmobile, a mountain biker, or hiker. Be respectful and careful. Although horses do tend to need the most accommodation because of their size and temperament, many of these other users have never encountered a horse before and might not know what to do. Because snowmobiles make a lot of noise, they might inadvertently scare your horse. If at all possible, move your horse far enough off the trail to let them safely pass. Most trail users find it fun to see a horse on the trail and wouldn't do anything intentional to scare your horse.

Endurance Rides

Endurance trail riding is for the hearty rider with a lot of time to spend conditioning both herself and the horse. Endurance trail rides are 50 to 100 miles long. Some endurance rides take as long as twenty-four hours, and riders start and finish in the dark, sometimes riding through the night. The horse must be in extremely good condition with great body weight, muscle tone, and wind stamina. And the horse must be very well trained with an ability to move out without being out of control. The idea is to spend the horse's energy covering ground, not to spend it fighting with the rider. The rider won't make it through the ride if she is struggling with her horse the entire time. Endurance rides are timed but it's also critical that the horse be "fit to continue" to win.

FACT

The Tevis Cup, formally called the Western States Trail Ride, is the most famous endurance ride in the United States, perhaps in the world. It has taken place in the Sierra high country near Lake Tahoe, Nevada, every August since 1955. The ride covers 100 miles in one day over rugged terrain. The winner is the horse/rider team that finishes in the shortest amount of time with a horse deemed "fit enough to continue." You can find out more about the Tevis Cup ride on the Web at *www.foothill.net/tevis*.

Special Equipment

As with every activity, trail riding has a whole complement of special equipment that you can purchase. Some of this equipment could make your ride more comfortable, particularly because there are some items you need to pack along for the ride.

Saddles are made that are designed for long-distance trail riding. They are light weight and have rings attached in various places around the saddle to clip things to it. Trail saddles also often have special wide stirrups that give the rider a nice comfortable foot rest, and they have a cushioned padding in the stirrup that helps with comfort in the long haul. Lastly, you can purchase seat covers for the saddle that pad or soften the seat for those long rides.

You want to wear very comfortable riding pants for long trail rides. Dress in layers and take time to add or remove layers to adjust to temperature changes. Bring along some sort of protective rain gear, especially if the temperatures are cool and rain is imminent.

You can clip water bottles, sponges, snack bags, and fanny packs to all those rings on the saddle. Even better than a water bottle is the water pack that straps to your back with a tube to drink from—those packs can be strapped down so they don't bounce around.

Depending on the trail surface conditions and the condition of your horse's feet, you might want to talk with your horseshoer about special shoes that have extra traction for rocky and high terrain. At the very least, be sure to tell your shoer that you are planning to do endurance or competitive trail riding with your horse.

If you are planning a tough trail ride, and especially if it includes trailering a long distance to strange country, give your horse an electrolyte supplement before, during, and after your trip. Electrolytes come in either paste form administered with a tube into the horse's mouth or in granular form that is sprinkled on the feed. These electrolytes provide essential minerals that the horse needs to maintain optimum body function and to encourage drinking. Always have fresh water available to the horse when he is given electrolytes. Add electrolytes to your own water supply also.

Chapter 16

Competition

Some riders spend their entire horse career competing in horse shows or other types of equestrian competition. They have fun; they meet a lot of like-minded people; and they find it challenging and rewarding. This chapter covers what you need to know to get started competing in horse shows.

What Is a Horse Show?

In its simplest form, a horse show is a venue for horses and riders to get together to show off their form or educational level and compete against other riders for ribbons and trophies. Shows aren't all the same—most vary in the types of classes they offer. Some local clubs might have a large population of miniature horses in their club members, and so they make sure their shows offer a group of classes for minis. Others have driving classes. Some clubs have enough interest in jumping that they take the time and money to create a separate jumping ring.

There are many competitions that don't call their events "shows." Team penning, reining, and trail rides all offer competitive events. Horse shows that focus on gamelike classes—barrel racing and pole bending, for example—are called "gymkhanas."

Lesson stables often offer students the opportunity to show their horses in competitions either right at the stable itself or on a show circuit that the stable follows. Being part of a show group from your lesson barn is a great way to learn about showing horses. You can have plenty of help in all aspects of showing. Your instructor will know what the current trends are in attire. You will learn everything from how to appropriately salute the judge in a dressage test to how to hold your nonreining hand in the Western pleasure class to the best way to get to the center of the ring for the end-of-class lineup. A really active barn with a great lesson program manager will bring in speakers, clinicians, and other presenters from whom you can learn all sorts of show information.

FACT

If you want to learn about showing your horse, the best way to start is by attending a lot of shows and just watching. Perhaps plan to compete at your first show toward the end of a season, after watching several shows throughout the early part of the show season. Watch different classes, pay attention to what riders are wearing; in other words, check out all aspects of it. Another way to get show experience is to volunteer; small riding clubs are always looking for warm bodies to help out.

The lesson barn that focuses on shows will help you have access to good horses for sale or lease that are educated in the discipline you are seeking to learn. Of course, you can do all this on your own, but you will have a learning curve to overcome, and it will take a lot longer and more experimentation to get to where you want to go.

The Show Circuit

Horse showing is comprised of formal "circuits." Typically, the farther afield you are willing to go to a show, the higher the level of the circuit you can compete in. If you show locally, the competition is less intense than if you show statewide, which is less intense than if you show regionally, which is less intense than the national circuit, and so on.

"Intensity" is based on the number of competitors as well as the caliber of the competitors and the course. In the highest levels of competition, horses are typically expensive and highly trained, and the riders have coaches and instructors, who work with them on the specific discipline they compete in.

ESSENTIAL

The show circuits are designated by letters of the alphabet; the higher the letter, the higher the level of circuit. Competing on the A-circuit means competing against top-quality horses and accomplished riders on premium courses built by the nation's top equestrian course designers. You shouldn't plan to start there, and you don't even have to aim for that high a level of showing! Some people show in the lower circuits for years and years because they are having fun.

The Local Circuit

The local circuit consists of those one-day, weekend horse shows that a local club sponsors. You join the club, and as a member, you compete in the club's horse shows. For the ribbons you win, you and your horse earn points. At the end of the year, there are "year-end awards" for members with the most points. Nonmembers can compete in the club's shows as well—anyone who follows the rules and is willing to the pay the entry fees can participate in the show—but nonmembers do not accumulate points.

Joining one of these small clubs can bring great benefits, such as riding companions, other riders to practice with, and just plain great friends who share a common interest. Some other perks often include access to the club's riding facility where they hold their shows and discounts at local businesses that affiliate with the club. Most clubs also hold year-end banquets where year-end awards and other prizes are handed out.

A local club is a fun way to focus your riding interest and to give yourself goals and keep things a little more interesting for your horse without too much pressure.

The Statewide Circuit

Showing on a state level often involves showing in your horse's breed association's state club. For instance, you might show in the Ohio Quarter Horse Association (OQHA) shows, competing with other horses and owners from the OQHA. Depending on the prevalence of the particular breed in your state, the statewide association can be large or small. The smaller the statewide association, the less likely it will sponsor many shows. At the state level, some clubs join together and have one show with specific classes where you can earn points in a particular circuit. For instance, in a state Quarter Horse show, there might be one or two classes where points can be earned for the state Paint Horse Association (PHA).

FACT

The Federation Equestre Internationale (FEI) is the international governing body for all Olympic equestrian sports and their qualifying competitions. The United States Equestrian Federation (USEF) is the national equivalent. Their Web sites are informative and comprehensive. Check them out at ✍www.horsesport.org and ✍www.usef.org, respectively.

Regional Circuits

Regional circuits take you a step higher than the statewide shows. Almost every region of the country—New England, the Mid-Atlantic, the Northwest—have regional horse showing circuits. Depending on the level of participation, the regional and statewide shows might be combined. Some regions are big enough so that it might require a bit of traveling to get there. The regional circuits are drawing from a larger pool of competitors and are therefore more challenging.

National and International Circuit

When you start to think about national and international show circuits, you are getting into the "big time" of showing. Don't expect to do this in one season! The competition is fierce, and you need to be on a high-level horse and have developed top-quality riding skills. You will need to have plenty of time to practice for the shows—making time every day—despite other commitments like jobs, spouse, and children. If you don't keep your horse at your home or you don't have the facility to practice properly, you will need access to a facility where you can practice regularly. And you definitely need a trainer, instructor, coach, or whatever you want to call the person who will be a mentor for you in learning all about showing.

If it interests you to show on the A-level circuits, by all means go for it! Just be realistic about the time and money it requires.

ALERT!

Just because you think showing in Western pleasure year after year after year is fun doesn't mean your horse does. Once your horse stops having fun, there's a good chance you aren't going to find it so much fun either. You will start to see behavioral issues and other indicators that are your horse telling you, "I'm bored!" Consider a change of discipline, a break, or even a change of horse. If you can't part with your current horse, keep him, get him out on the trails, and lease a different one for the show.

Horse Show Classifications

Horse show classes are classified by what the judges are judging. Some judge just the horse; some just the rider; and some judge trail-riding ability.

Pleasure Class

Horse show classes that are called "pleasure," whether they are English pleasure or Western pleasure, are judged on the horse's performance. They usually consist of walk, trot, canter one direction, then the other. Of course, your horse won't show very well if you are pounding around all over his back, losing you stirrups, and can't get him into the canter. But the judging itself is based on how nicely your horse goes and how quickly he responds to your commands.

Equitation Class

Equitation class is the opposite of pleasure class—this class is judged solely on the rider's riding ability, i.e., "equitation." Again, even though the judging is focused on only one half the team, the horse has to help you look good. If your horse has a naturally bouncy trot, and you haven't either helped him learn to compose his trot or haven't learned how to sit to it, you simply won't look very polished. Equitation classes usually require you to ride a specific pattern. Equitation classes can involve more than just riding around the ring both ways; there are also jumping equitation classes where your jumping form is judged.

Trail Class

Trail class is where you can combine your pleasure and equitation with some obstacles tossed in. You need to ride correctly, give your horse the cues he needs to navigate an obstacle, and often there are places where you are expected to do a specified gait from one obstacle to the next.

It's up to the competitor to learn the patterns for any classes that call for them. Each class, including trail class, jumping class, equitation, and showmanship (in hand) class, often includes a pattern for you and your horse to perform. If you have signed up for such classes, find out when the pattern will be posted and go look at it as soon as possible. Figure out some memory tricks to help you remember the pattern. And look at the course if at all possible.

The Show Horse

Any horse can be entered in a horse show. You don't have to purchase a hugely expensive horse that has a string of show credits on his resume. But there are certain horses that are better suited to horse show life. And if you decide to use old Dobbin, he will need some tuning up and some instruction in how to fit into the horse show ring.

Learning Together

If you have the time, the discipline, and access to a good teacher, you and your horse can learn the show circuit together. Pick a discipline that interests you or one that your horse seems to be suited for (preferably both of those criteria!) and get started. Spend time at the kind of competitions you plan to ride in. See what your horse will need to do to be competitive. And then practice. And practice. And practice some more. Enter a show, see how you do, and then practice, practice, practice to make it to the next level.

The "Made" Horse

Sometimes the best way to learn about showing is when one of you— either you or your horse—are veterans. A horse that already knows how to perform in the B-circuit Western pleasure ring, or over 3'6" jumps would be a great teacher to take you through the lower level show circuit or get you started on the 3' jump course.

This doesn't mean you don't need to practice ahead of time. Horses are live animals that respond differently to the feel presented to them by each and every rider and handler who comes their way. You want to know that the two of you have a rapport before you go flying over the jumps in the show ring.

Purchasing an accomplished show horse might be beyond your budget. And even if you could afford the price, you might find that it doesn't take too long before you are wanting to do more than just be along for the ride. If you catch the horse-showing bug, you will get the desire to teach a horse how to be successful in the show ring. Consider leasing a show veteran for a season or two. This will give you time to learn the ropes. Once you know what you are doing, you can become the veteran member of your team and purchase or lease a horse that is not as familiar with showing.

FACT

Animals grow "winter coats" not in response to the cold, as is commonly thought, but actually in response to the shortening of the daylight hours. Therefore, horses grow winter coats no matter what part of the country they live in.

Getting Ready for Show Season

Even regions of the country that don't go into riding hibernation for the cold months of the winter have a down season. The "show season" typically runs from April through October or November. The later months are often reserved for the year-end championship shows. And in the Snowbelt, the beginning of the season might not come until May.

Whichever region you live in, you should plan to give your horse a break from the show ring. Perhaps between Thanksgiving and the new year is a great time to let him just kick up his heels and maybe take you on a quiet trail ride through the woods once or twice a week. By around February, however, if you plan to seriously compete in the upcoming show season, you should be starting your conditioning program.

Like you would do for yourself if you were going to engage in physical exercise, build your horse up gradually. Develop a plan for the season that will include an increasing amount of exercise from the time you begin working him again to the time he begins showing.

Almost before the last show season is over, you will want to make some decisions about blanketing, clipping, and artificial lighting. All these things have an impact on how polished your horse will look at the beginning of the show season. Serious artificial lighting will reduce the thickness of his winter coat, but this is probably more than the average show competitor will want to do, and it's really not quite fair to the horse. Clipping will allow you to work the horse in the winter without him sweating profusely under his heavy winter coat. But if you clip, you will need to use blankets to give him an artificial coat to replace the natural one he doesn't have. Blanketing is a fine art, requiring layering and/or different blanket weights to be really effective. And if you board your horse, there might be a surcharge to put blankets on and take them off every day.

Other Competitions

There are plenty of other ways to be competitive with your horse besides the traditional horse shows. There are a wealth of competitive opportunities for trail riders. But the excitement doesn't end there. Some competitions are traditional, and others are just becoming popular.

Polo

Polo has been around almost as long as humans have been riding horses. And it's one of the few equestrian competitions that is a team sport. Polo is basically hockey while riding on horses with a grass rink. Two teams of four players compete against each other in a round of six "chukkers" that each last seven and a half minutes. Outdoor polo is played on a huge open field of 160 yards by 300 yards.

More manageable is "arena polo" that is played either in or out of doors with a field size of just 150 feet by 300 feet. Indoor polo is played with only three players per team and only three chukkers.

To play polo competitively, you need a good deal of riding experience under your belt! Although outdoor polo is a much faster sport than arena polo, both are fast, exciting, so you need good balance, and you have to be willing to canter a lot.

Doing polo at all competitively requires that you are living in an area where the sport is organized—or you can start your own club! To find out everything you might want to know about polo, click onto the United States Polo Association's Web site, *www.us-polo.org*. You will find the rules on the Web site and learn how to locate a club near you.

Competing should be rewarding and a learning experience. You can expect to get a few butterflies in your stomach the night before a show or moments before you enter a class, but if it stresses you out beyond all reason, it's not worth it! Use competition to compete against yourself— if you haven't won a ribbon yet this season, go to the show with the goal of placing. The next time, the goal can be to place higher than you did before. Don't come home from the show depressed because you didn't win all blue ribbons. The idea is to have fun and some reason to practice your riding skills.

Polocrosse

Polocrosse, like it sounds, is a combination of polo and lacrosse. Instead of mallets, players carry a lacrosse-like net. This variation on polo is becoming very popular.

Team Penning

Born from ranch work, team penning is another equestrian team sport. In team penning, teams of three riders attempt to sort a group of cattle out of a small herd and get them into a pen at one end of the arena in less time than the other competitors. But the sorting out is not just any of the cattle—the team picks a number before they enter the arena to compete, and they need to sort and pen the cows with that number on them. Each team member has a job to do, from sorting to holding the cows back from a "foul line," to holding the cows in the pen while the others are being sorted and brought to the pen. It's typically great fun and could be as fast or slow as the level and skill of the club. The hardest part about being involved in team penning is that cows are hard to come by in some parts of the country. For the competition to remain fun and the horses to remain interested, you need to have a steady supply of fresh cattle.

Jousting

Jousting is the official state sport of the state of Maryland! The sport has had a great revival in part due to the popularity of Renaissance Festivals. Don't worry, you don't have to impale your fellow competitors or knock them off their horses. Jousting is essentially an independent sport where each competitor attempts to lance a series of rings that each hang from the cross bar of an "arch." Time and the number of rings you lance determine the winner. You need to be willing to ride very fast and accurately position your horse to get the ring to be successful at jousting. Check out ✎*www.nationaljousting.com* to learn all about this sport on the National Jousting Association's Web site.

Cowboy Mounted Shooting

Another sport that has become increasingly popular within the last decade is called Cowboy Mounted Shooting. As with polo and jousting, you need to ride fast and accurately and to successfully shoot (blanks) at targets (usually balloons) placed at intervals along the course. Many competitors even dress up in old Western-style costumes to give the contest the full cowboy effect.

QUESTION?

I think I would like to compete in horse shows, but I don't ride very well. How well do you have to ride to enter a show?

There are no minimum requirements to ride in a general horse show, but in more specific shows like jumping, you might have to prove some level of proficiency to compete at each level. You can work your way up. Start out in the "walk, trot" classes or the "novice" or "amateur" divisions, and work your way up. The judge and how you place in the ribbons (if you place) could help you assess how you are progressing.

Chapter 17

Focus on Kids

Kids love horses. Many horseback riding lesson programs revolve around the younger set. You might be a horse-owning parent and want to get your kids involved. Or horses might be completely mysterious and intimidating to you, but you feel like it's time to fulfill your child's growing desire to ride. Either way, there are a lot of factors to keep in mind—safety, cost, time—but being around horses can have such great positive effects on kids that if your child is interested, it's worth investigating.

Kids Learning to Ride

Kids can gain a lot more than just enjoyment from learning to ride horses. Successful equine experiences help boost their self-confidence, which benefits all areas of their lives. Imagine being less than 3 feet tall but having the ability to accurately maneuver an animal like a horse! It's a great feeling.

A Stable Focused on Kids

Whether you are looking for a boarding stable where your child can board her new horse or a stable where she can take regular riding lessons, find one that is focused on kids. In a stable where kids are the focus, your child will interact a lot with other kids. Often the stable holds its own small horse shows or is the site for sponsoring larger horse shows. Also, the stable might have a trailer and take a certain number of kids around to show circuits in the area where the kids could compete on a local or regional basis.

Stables focused on kids usually have extensive summer programs where kids can spend lots of time there during summer vacation from school. The instructors are often hired because of their experience with teaching children. And the horses used for lessons have been picked with kids in mind. The stable is organized so that it's as safe for kids as it is for adults. The stable provides kids with lots of lessons in safety.

QUESTION?

My daughter's instructor has started putting her on much larger horses as she's improved as a rider. Is this okay, or is she safer on smaller horses?

While it's true that if you fall off the trip to the ground is farther on a taller horse, safety on horses has little to do with the size of the horse. A good instructor will always balance the level of the horse's and rider's education. If you have had great confidence in her instructor over these two or three years, then you can probably continue to trust the instructor's judgment. But you should always feel comfortable talking with your daughter's instructor about exactly these kinds of issues.

If there are several options in your area, then you can start to choose a stable whose riding focus is what your child is interested in. If she's not yet sure what type of riding she's interested in, try them all before committing to one! Keep in mind that if your child decides she doesn't like Western or she gets bored with it, she can always switch to the stable that focused on jumping or on cow working and reining.

A stable that is set up to give lessons to kids should have plenty of kid-sized equipment around. It's not safe to learn to ride horses in saddles that are too big or too small. English saddle stirrups tend to be completely adjustable to any length leg. The stirrups on Western saddles are a little less adjustable, and so it's even more important to have a child's saddle where the stirrups are already pretty short.

ESSENTIAL

Look for a stable that involves the kids in more than just riding. Things like grooming, health care, feeding, costs, and stall cleaning are all important things for horse-crazy kids to learn about. Some stables that focus on children's lessons also have a "classroom" portion of the lesson. It's important for kids to learn that being involved with horses isn't just about riding.

Lessons for Kids

Kids typically get more enjoyment and learn more out of group lessons than individual lessons. Whether this is possible depends on the size of the facility you find. To be able to give group lessons, a stable needs to have several ponies/small horses and enough equipment for several of them to be ridden at the same time.

It will depend on what's available within range of your home (or your kid's school and/or your office), but if you are willing to drive far enough, you can find kids' lesson programs in almost any equine discipline from jumping to learning to show to trail riding.

Camps for Kids

Some summer camps for kids have horseback riding available to the kids who want to ride. Some kids' summer camps revolve completely around horseback riding. These can be just day camps that last for six weeks of the summer, or they can be overnight programs where your child goes off for two weeks and is involved in all-horses-all-the-time for those two weeks. Most camps focus the learning and teaching by leading up to something like an end-of-camp horse show where families are invited to come and watch. This kind of horse absorption can be great fun for kids.

Safety

Of course, if a child has an exceptionally bad experience with horses, his self-confidence, at least when it comes to horses, can go the other way. Accidents are bound to happen, but with the right child-focused safety precautions, barns can reduce the chances that accidents will be serious ones. That's where it becomes critical to pick a safe barn whose instructors consider safety above all else. Look for a place for your child to take lessons with the following things in mind.

Appropriate-sized Horses

Horses used in a children's lesson program should be of appropriate size for kids. Ponies under 14 hands are much more suited for young kids to learn to ride on. The kid could gain a lot more confidence when he is in proportion with his mount. When the kid rides a horse that he needs to climb to the top of the fence to get on and from whom the ground is so far, the kid might feel the need for a parachute to dismount. An older child or a child who is tall for her age can be safely mounted on a full-sized horse on the smaller side of 15 hands. But don't fall for that old attitude of being impressed by the huge 16.3 hand Warmblood that petite eight-year-old Suzy can handle. Again, it might be okay once Suzy has developed her seat and has had a couple of years of riding confidence under her belt. But you want to stack the deck in her favor so that she will maintain her interest for those two years—and she won't if she is totally intimidated. Don't expect all kids to admit that they are intimidated, if the kid is new to riding, she might have no idea what to expect.

FACT

You might imagine your daughter and her horse as a classy package, and the fuzzy Thelwell cartoon that comes to mind when you think "pony" just doesn't fit the bill. A pony is simply the official name for an equine that is under 14.2 hands. So a 14.1 hand pony with a young person astride can look quite like a full-sized horse and adult rider! There are "pony breeds" that are genetically evolved to be small, and then there are pony-sized animals in almost every breed.

Safe Horses

You can talk to ten different people and get ten different answers as to the qualities of a safe horse. In the final analysis, nothing guarantees safety with horses. But again, you want to be sure the lesson barn is stacking the deck in your child's favor.

A key thing to do is to watch your child's lesson regularly. Don't be afraid to speak up if you see something you think looks unsafe! It might just be something you don't understand, and the instructor might be able to explain what is going on. But it's your prerogative as a parent to oversee your child's safety. If a barn makes you or your concerns seem unwelcome, find another lesson barn for your child. Be careful before something happens that you would have spoken up about had you felt like anyone would listen.

So what kinds of things do make one horse more safe than another? Many people think age is a huge factor. A horse under three is perhaps too young for a beginning child. But it's really not the age itself, it's the horse's education that is the issue; there are plenty of teenaged horses who are ridden all the time and remain pretty uneducated.

With age can simply come experience—a horse that has "been there, done that" can be much more safe for a child who is learning to ride. Many lesson programs comprise champion-level horses that have had great success in the show ring for many years but finally soured on the show circuit. These horses can be quite happy packing a child around a ring for a one-hour lesson. But that same horse might not be appropriate for a child to take out on the trail. Trail riding can be so foreign to a show horse that they freak out at every little noise and need an experienced, supportive rider to feel okay being out of the ring.

ALERT!

Beware the instructor with the "militant" style of teaching. Kids don't need this! Part of the point of being involved with horses is the fun. Unless your child is headed for Olympic competition, the drill sergeant approach can turn kids off rather than challenge them. Kids are often challenged to do well when they really like their instructor and want to make him proud of them.

The Instructor

A safety-oriented instructor is a must. How can you tell when an instructor is focusing her lesson program on safety? The instructor will be constantly doing and saying things that relate to safety such as constantly reminding students that not only do all mounted riders have to have a helmet on, the helmet must be buckled as well. You will see her check the girth of each rider's saddle before starting the lesson. A good instructor will know how to challenge kids without making them feel totally overwhelmed and intimidated. And key to a good instructor is someone who is not afraid to change her approach when something clearly isn't working.

Apparel for Kids

One of the difficult things with kids when they need specific clothing to do something like horseback riding is that they have this funny thing about growing! This is where used clothing can come in real handy. Many tack shops have a used section. Most of the kids stuff will probably be in great condition because kids often don't have coats and pants long enough to really ruin them—they grow out of them first! For just plain riding, your child won't need anything fancy. A good pair of jeans and a good pair of boots can probably easily be found used. If special clothes are needed for the show circuit, definitely search the used racks.

Photograph by Bob Atkins

▲ Kids can learn a lot from horseback riding.

However, the one item of clothing you should not buy used is a helmet. Spring for a new, quality helmet. The helmet manufacturers include inserts to make a larger-sized helmet fit a smaller-sized head so a helmet for a kid can last two or three years. Don't buy a used helmet—you have no idea if the former owner took a spill with it and once a helmet saves your head it should be discarded or sent back to the manufacturer for replacement.

Kids and Competition

As a parent, you have probably already had to figure out how you want to deal with your children and their attitudes toward competition. Kids can be very competitive—and they can also learn how to show good sportsman-ship as well!

One thing that makes horse competition a little different is that all impor-tant, hard to ignore factor: the horse. This huge live animal brings a different slant to competition as kids might know it. Few equine competitive events are team events like other sports kids might have already been involved with. And they need to learn how to work with their horse in a way that makes the horse a willing partner in the competition. It can be very chal-lenging and very rewarding!

FACT

Look for a barn for your child to take lessons at that also requires students to learn about all aspects of horse care. They should learn how to groom and tack up their own horse. They should also learn about feeding, stall cleaning, and other important things. Kids get to learn a lot more about what it takes to have a horse this way and can have a better understand-ing of why perhaps they can't have their own horse at the moment.

Buying a Horse for Your Child

Chances are that for a horse-crazy kid, almost any horse you would buy would be the best horse on earth. But if the child is going to really love this animal and be the one taking care of and riding him, she should be involved in the purchase. Make a deal ahead of time that you will be looking at several horses before buying one. A horse-crazy girl is going to fall in love with the first horse you look at, almost without question. So if you go into it knowing that you will definitely look at five more before deciding, you'll soon learn that she will fall in love with horse number two, three, four, five, and six as well!

See the Horse Ridden

Always have someone else ride the horse first so you can see how the horse acts under saddle—after all, for kids, riding is often the most impor-tant part. Where adults can take more pleasure in learning along with the horse and find as much reward from grooming and caring for the horse, kids want to get on and ride, ride, ride!

Always bring your child's helmet along when you are shopping for horses. It's best to have someone else ride the horse first and see how he behaves under saddle before you put your child up there. But if you are serious about the horse, then your daughter or son should try him out. A child needs to be comfortable with the horse or you will find that going to the barn is something you have to convince the kid to do.

Behavior Issues

Behavioral issues are not always a reason not to buy a horse. Horses respond to the feel they get from their handler. If the handler makes the horse feel defensive, the horse might have some issues that could be reversed under a different handler and with some effort. Some horses learn to play a little game of tag before they let you catch them in the pen—they aren't dangerous or disrespectful necessarily, they either just think this is what they are supposed to do or they simply find it fun! A lot of what you can deal with on the behavioral issue front has a lot to do with your and/or your child's level of experience. Don't buy a horse that lunges at you when you come into the stall or paddock—who needs that to deal with? A horse that is hard to catch or moves when being mounted or is difficult to bridle, isn't necessarily dangerous. Find some experienced help to get you and your child beyond those difficulties.

FACT

Self-confidence is just one of the many things that horses can teach people, especially kids. Kids can learn about the fruits of hard work. They can learn about the cost of things and how to save for what they want. They can learn about trade-offs—like time in the barn in exchange for time at the homework assignment. And they can learn things like time management and efficiency. The list is endless!

Home or Board?

If your child's horse will live at your home and the child will be responsible for the horse's care, she will need to have some adult supervision. She might love the horse more than anything, but she is still a child who isn't yet experienced enough in life to fully appreciate how much that the horse depends on her!

Chances are she will be in the barn with her horse every waking moment she is allowed to be. Give her all the responsibility for caring for the horse but, unless you are into horses too and are in the barn every day anyway, make a point to check in on things regularly. Is the horse being fed? How often do you need to go get a supply of hay and grain? Does the horse look healthy with a nice coat and no ribs showing?

ALERT!

Since horses' mouths are on the ground a lot picking up more than just grass, horses need to be regularly dewormed, usually every two to three months. The simplest way is to use a paste product that comes in a tube marked with weight increments. It's simple enough for kids to do but even though most dewormers are very safe for the animals they are made for, they are not safe for humans or other animals so make sure the tubes are disposed of immediately!

Boarding a horse somewhere brings a whole new aspect to life. Find a place you are comfortable at because you will be there more than you realize! You'll come to pick Ernie up at the stable only to find the lesson is running late. Or Suzy please, please, please wants just fifteen more minutes to finish braiding Scarlet's mane. Or the instructor really wants to show you how well Brett is doing on the 2'6" jumps.

If you live in cold climates, look for a place with an indoor arena with a heated viewing room and preferably also a heated lounge area because horse activity goes on rain or shine, cold or hot. Get yourself a pair of sturdy boots that you wear only to the boarding stable.

When choosing a boarding stable, cheapest is not always best. You need to decide what will work best for your child. If she is a beginner, she will need not only riding lessons but you will want to make sure someone is around to help teach her how to care for a horse. Sometimes it can be great to have a small situation where, say, the neighbor a half a mile away has a horse and has room to board another in return for a modest amount of money and some stall cleaning. But if the neighbor is going to charge almost as much as a stable with an indoor arena, the place with the arena might work better. You don't want to spend money on your daughter's horse and have her only ride him six months out of the year.

Chapter 18

E Try Something Different!

Perhaps you are simply looking for something new to do with your horse or perhaps you are looking to do something more organized. Some of these "different" things to become involved in with horseback riding are common horseback riding activities that might not seem so common to you. Others are unusual. All are fun!

Polocrosse

This exciting sport is first on the list since it's a great activity for novice riders. Polocrosse has been used for practically centuries as a sport for new riders to learn how to ride. Not as intense as polo, polocrosse allows riders to have fun and stop concentrating so hard—before you know it, you are in tune with your horse and you aren't even trying.

Polocrosse has many similarities to its sister sport, polo. The game is played on a grass or dirt field approximately 160 yards long and 60 yards wide with 10-foot high goal posts at each end. Like polo, the game is played in six- to eight-minute time periods called "chukkers." Games are umpired, keeping things organized and fair. Some significant differences are that the game is much less intense and you can use one horse for the entire game.

You'll need to have a hornless saddle (Australian saddles are often used) plus a helmet and a lacrosse-like racquet. And a horse to ride, of course! Your horse will need bell boots and protective leg wraps.

Polocrosse is played with two teams, each with three players on the field at a time. Each team has three relief players as well.

If you can't locate a polocrosse club in your area, consider starting one of your own! Check the American Polocrosse Association Web site at *www.americanpolocrosse.org.*

FACT

It's not necessary to jump in full tilt with a new activity. Go watch a polocrosse tournament or a team penning and get a sense of whether the type of horseback riding required and the kind of people it attracts is something that really would interest you enough to become involved.

Polo

Polo is probably best left to the advanced rider, but as far as learning the game, you have to start somewhere. Each team member needs several horses to carry them through one of these intense games.

Set up similarly to polocrosse, polo is played on a long field with goals at either end. Instead of a racket, you use a long mallet. Observe a polo match or two, and you will see that horses need to be quick and tolerant of a lot of activity, including things like the rider leaning way off the saddle, perhaps at a gallop!

You might be surprised to find pockets of polo playing not far from you. If not, the United States Polo Association Web site tells everything you need to know to start your own club (*www.us-polo.org*). Polo is played at the high school and college level. Although thought of as a sport for the rich, polo clubs often offer lessons that are designed to be a low-key entry into the sport.

If you have become a balanced rider and love a fast pace, give polo a try, it might be just the horse sport you are looking for.

Like any new horse activity you are considering, don't run out and spend money on all the equipment you need before you are certain you will enjoy the activity. Borrow equipment or make do with what you have. Once you know you will stay involved for a while, you can start to accumulate your own made-for-the-sport items.

Cow Work

Horses respond to cows. Working with cows is a great way to get your horse interested in his work while you refine his skills and get the two of you working together better. Obviously if you ride in an English saddle, you can't rope a cow and dally without a horn (and even then you should have a roping saddle and lots of roping lessons!). But you can certainly work a cow along the fence in an English saddle. It's not about equipment, it's about horsemanship.

There are several possibilities for working cows with your horse. If you get involved in an organized cow-related activity, you will want to have the proper equipment and that is Western-style equipment. A Western saddle is more suited to keep you in place when the horse moves unpredictably with the unpredictable movements of the cow.

Team penning is popular and events and clubs are found almost everywhere in the country. Team penning involves a team of three riders. The team pulls a number prior to entering an arena where a group of numbered cows await. The team's job is to sort the right numbered cows out of the group and work them to the empty pen. One member of the team moves the cow while another team rider discourages the cow from going back to the herd and the third team member holds the team's cows as they collect in the pen.

Team penning clubs are often local groups who just have fun a couple of nights a week.

Entire competitions in the show ring revolve around cow work as well. Cutting and working cattle along the fence line. Cow working classes are not regularly found in local and smaller shows. If you and a few friends are interested in working cows with your horses, you can sometimes find a source of a few cows that you can rent once in a while.

If you can, find someone who knows about working cattle with horses to help you. Many horse clinics offer cow working classes. It's important to learn the best way to introduce your horse to cows to help it remain intrigued, not frightened of or bored by them. There are other things to learn, like how a horse rates a cow, never turn your horse away from the cow, and other seemingly small things that are big things to your horse.

ALERT!

Many fun horse activities can be organized by gathering a group of riders together a couple of times a week. Although keeping things simple is an admirable goal, getting a little more formally organized with some rules and regulations can help avoid controversies.

Jousting

The medieval activity of jousting is making a comeback. Don't worry—instead of running at each other with long spears, jousting is now typically an individual sport. The jouster does have a spear of sorts, but the spear catches rings hanging from an apparatus known as an "arch."

The 10-foot-wide arches on a jousting track are spaced around 30 yards apart. There are three arches and the track length is 160 yards, allowing for space on either end to gain speed and to slow your horse down. The event is timed, with the standard time to run the track at nine seconds!

Although jousting is the state sport of Maryland and their association has been around since 1950, the sport is not popular enough for there to be standard equipment you can purchase. One of the fun things about jousting is that everything is homemade and therefore each course is unique. All you need are arches, rings, and lances.

The object of modern-day jousting is to spear the rings hanging from the arches at the fastest speed that you can. Each contestant gets three rounds, called "charges," to get a potential total of nine rings. The winner is the rider who has ridden within the standard time and has the most rings. There is then a tie-breaking charge if necessary. If the game is still tied at this point, the rings get reduced in size!

To find out more about the game, check the National Jousting Association Web site at *www.nationaljousting.com*.

It might be difficult to find "unusual" horse activities happening in your area. If that's the case, the next best thing is to spark interest yourself! Put up some flyers in horse places like tack shops and boarding barns and see if you can get a group together to start a jousting or polocrosse club. Start small at first—you want this to be about riding horses and having fun not about keeping track of paperwork and membership. Once you have things figured out—the rules of your chosen sport, a place to play, etc.—then you can open it up to more people.

Fox Hunting

Although foxes are no longer involved in fox hunting, horses and dogs, protocols, and rituals certainly are. If fox hunting really intrigues you, you probably won't have to travel too far to hitch up with a hunt club. There are nine recognized hunt clubs in New England alone. The season typically runs from August through the end of the year, depending, in the cold climates, on how long the weather and footing holds out.

The first few weeks of the hunting season is known as "cubbing." In present-day hunts, this is when novices and children can ride along and learn the rules. Speak with the club president to find out more about how to join the club. As a guest and/or novice, you will ride in the rear after all club members have gone out.

Plan to dress smartly and conservatively! Dark coat, gloves, and white breeches are safe bets. The scarlet-colored jackets that seem to signify fox hunting are allowed to be worn only by the hunt staff and to the huntsmen who have been "awarded colors." Helmets are almost certainly required by all clubs and are a standard piece of attire.

In a nutshell, a member of the club drags a fox-scented rag along a trail. The dogs are let loose and the riders follow. At the end of the trail, all are rewarded with a lovely (usually potluck) lunch and/or tea.

FACT

Fox hunting has its roots in Great Britain. While it didn't come to North America on the *Mayflower*, it wasn't much longer after that when hounds were reportedly imported to the New World. George Washington is believed to have partaken in the sport. Fox hunting has given birth to hundreds of lovely collectible trinkets from "stirrup cups" that held the end-of-the-hunt alcoholic fortification to decorative items portraying various aspects of the hunt.

Re-enactments

If you liked to play dress-up as a child, here's your chance to carry that trait into adulthood. Re-enactments are serious business and there are several that involve horses.

Civil War

Civil War re-enactments are perhaps the most well organized—and you don't have to go to Gettysburg for them. Any field can become a Civil War battlefield. No one dies, of course, and no one should get hurt. This is make believe, even though the members are very serious about authenticity and the accuracy of the re-enactment.

Your horse will probably need to be patient and calm, since their role in a re-enactment will not include much running around. He also should be pretty well exposed to things like flags, drums, and even cannons going off as well as lots of people milling around him.

For a list of Civil War re-enactments around the country, check out the Fort Tyler Web site at *www.forttyler.com*.

Renaissance Faires

Renaissance faires, called "renfaires" for short, have long been popular in Europe but have become more prevalent in the United States as well. If the romance of knights and dragons and fair maidens sounds like fun to you, get thee to a renfaire!

Renaissance faires of the sixteenth century were celebrations that reveled in the end of winter. Food, crafts, games, and those gallant knights were all in abundance then and continue to be in today's renaissance faire re-enactments.

The Web site *www.renaissance-faire.com* lists faires all around the United States. And there are many! Not all have horse events, but many do. After all, what is a renaissance faire without a knight on his trusty steed?

You don't need to own your own costume to be in a re-enactment. Check out the local costume rental shop. They might even be able to tell you the names of groups that are doing re-enactments, which are organized from New Hampshire to California.

Cowboy Mounted Shooting

This unusual horse activity is growing in popularity fast. You can find most everything you want to know at *www.cowboymountedshooting.com* but suffice it to say the faster and smoother you can ride, the more adept you'll be at this sport. Your horse needs to learn to be calm at the sound of a gun being shot from his back (don't worry, the bullets are blanks). The Web site offers some tips on training your horse to accept your shooting.

To compete, you basically ride your horse as fast as you can and still be accurate at shooting a series of targets, often balloons. The rider with the best time and the most hit targets wins. Penalties are given for missing your target, running the course wrong, and falling off your horse! Safety is emphasized at all times.

As with the other unusual sports mentioned in this chapter, the Cowboy Mounted Shooting Association offers lots of information on starting up a club yourself if you can't find one in your area.

ALERT!

Fair warning—many of these offbeat horse activities are the type that are done at full throttle! But if you start your own club, whether it's jousting or polocrosse, you can choose to have a walk-trot only club or a walk-trot division that novices can enjoy. It often takes more skill to keep your horse at a trot in an exciting activity than it does to rip down the course. And if your horse has had a good foundation of bending well and stopping crisply, you will be whacking the polo ball toward your goal while your competitor is flying past the goal post trying to stop her horse!

Parades

Getting your horse "parade-broke" is an exercise in good horsemanship in and of itself! Unless you have a lot of experience working with horses that are pretty fired up, here is another instance where it would be best to call upon Old Faithful.

You will need some help from some horse friends you trust to get your horse exposed to the kinds of things he will experience if he is in a parade. People usually give a horse a pretty wide berth, but it's important in the parade environment that he learn not to kick at things as his first reaction!

One of the things your friends can do is simply expose him to a lot of activity going on around him all at once.

Take it in stages. Start with a group of people milling around slowly. Then have them mill around a little faster. Then maybe add a few people. And add then some items like small flags and balloons. Then move up to perhaps a makeshift drum or other loud musical instrument.

QUESTION?

I am interested in doing something fun with horses but I don't own a horse. How can I join an activity like polocrosse without my own horse?

Many "unusual" horse activities recognize that a lot of people who don't own horses are interested in riding and joining a club. And the clubs are very interested in promoting their sport. One thing you can do is volunteer to help out at events—small groups always need volunteer help. That way you can get to know the group members, and they can get to know you as a responsible, dedicated person. Also, many of these groups offer lessons to novices on horses that they provide.

Give your horse lots of breaks. If he is wild, forget it, and either come back to it another time, wait until he's had more life experience, or choose another horse. If he's concerned but not wild, he's going to look to you for support. This is a great opportunity for you to come through for him and step your relationship up a notch. Pat him, talk to him, ride him confidently, and he will think you are the best thing in the world to be near in a scary situation.

When you feel you and your horse are ready for some real parade action, don't skip Thanksgiving dinner and head to downtown Manhattan for the Macy's parade! Start with the small parade in a small town nearby. There are always plenty of "move-up" opportunities when it comes to parades.

Chapter 19

Horseback Riding on Vacation

For those who enjoy horseback riding, literally hundreds, perhaps thousands of opportunities abound in the United States to ride. Expand your horizons to Europe, Australia, and other more exotic destinations and the choices are limitless.

Bring Your Horse or Rent One?

You could haul a horse from state to state to state and always find more gorgeous country with organized trails. But you certainly don't need to bring or even own your own horse. You can reach a public horseback riding stable with horses for rent within a short distance of almost anywhere you choose to vacation.

In most cases, your skill level doesn't matter. In fact, if you do have horseback riding experience sometimes it pays not to mention it—then they won't stick you on the gelding nicknamed Bucks-Once-in-a-While or the mare they secretly call Runs-Away-If-Given-Her-Head.

If you plan to ride on your vacation, it helps to bring a pair of shoes that are suitable for riding safely. If you are planning to ride often or for long (half day or more) trips, bring your own helmet too. Most stables that rent horses have a collection of helmets for riders to wear and some require it; that's fine if you are going on one one-hour ride during your whole ten-day vacation. But it's always nice to have your own safety equipment that fits you and is comfortable.

FACT

Don't forget, when you decide to bring your horse along on a vacation, you are packing for two! Think ahead to every possible situation that might arise (and even some you can't imagine). Pack a couple of horse blankets of different weights, leg wraps for an unexpected injury, a first aid kit, flashlight, and extra batteries. Put some food in the truck for both you and your horse. Be prepared and hope you won't need most of it.

Traveling with Your Horse

Plan to make some short trips with your horse if you don't have a lot of experience driving a horse trailer. It's always best—and usually lots more fun—to go on a horse traveling vacation with a friend. That means there is always someone to hold horses if the other person needs to fix something.

Pack everything you can fit in—if you are hauling a horse trailer then you have a truck so fill it up! You can never have enough warm clothes, extra snacks, or water for your horse. Even an extra saddle in case something breaks on one (although you will have carefully cleaned and checked your tack before your trip). Make sure you leave yourself and your riding companion plenty of room to be comfortable but fill up the rest of the space with stuff you might be glad you have when you are waiting out a rainstorm or stuck on the side of the highway in a traffic jam.

ALERT!

Although most rental horse riding stables don't care if you're wearing riding shoes or your bedroom slippers, you need to look out for your own safety. Even though most rental horses at riding stables are so dull they just plod along the trail barely aware you are up there, there is always an element of potential danger when you are riding a horse.

Some Things to Consider

One thing to keep in mind when bringing your own horse is that the parks are wary of nonnative hay that carries weeds that are not native to the area. They prefer that you bring either weed-free hay or use "complete feeds" that have concentrated hay. Most parks do not allow grazing in any areas; you should avoid that anyway since you might not know the native plants that are poisonous to horses.

Always learn all the rules of a particular park before you go with your own horse. If you rent horses from a stable within the park, they will be sure you understand all the important rules before you ride out. Be sure to use hitching posts where they are available to avoid damaging the park's trees by tying a horse to them.

And always clean up after yourself, both your own litter and your horse's manure and feed droppings. This is especially important in trailhead parking areas that are often tight for parking and have high usage. Bring a manure bucket and fork to move manure out of the parking areas.

When you are checking out your hauling vehicle before a bring-your-own-horse vacation, don't forget to check the trailer too. Check tire air pressure, signal lights, and the trailer's emergency brake battery. Have the bearings greased at least once every year or two. Pull the floor mats up and check the floor boards. Fix the little things that might have broken and that would be more frustrating on a long trip.

National Parks

The U.S. National Park System alone offers hundreds of opportunities to ride horses in almost every park in the system. Here are a dozen highlights from coast to coast.

FACT

If something intrigues you in the list of national park riding opportunities, you can find more detailed information by checking the National Park Service Web site (*www.nps.gov*) and searching "horseback riding" or by sending for literature from the U.S. National Park Service, Department of the Interior, 1849 C Street NW, Washington, DC 20240.

Acadia National Park

This park on the beautiful Maine coast is a highly horse-friendly park. Stables and campsites are available. John D. Rockefeller made a gift of the extraordinary 57-mile carriage driving trails, making carriage driving especially prominent in this park while at the same time making the park horse-friendly. No horses are available for rental, you need to bring your own, but the horse and human accommodations make that easy, comfortable, and affordable.

Gettysburg National Park

What more poignant way to tour the Gettysburg Battlefields in south central Pennsylvania than via horseback? Two facilities, Cornerstone Farm (888) 334-8205; *www.cornerstonefarmbandb.com* and Hickory Hollow Farm (717) 224-0349; *www.hickoryhollowfarm.com* offer guided rides for all levels of riders through the park.

Assateague Island National Seashore

Since AINP is located in both Virginia and Maryland, riding can get a little complicated but it does offer three riding areas. You can trailer your own horse but you need to know the rules. Mostly, riding is permitted in Off-Road Vehicle (ORV) areas. You are only permitted to ride during the "winter season," after or before the biting fly season begins since there are many insect-transmittable horse diseases in the summer months. Carry your horse's water with you, and be sure to bring clean-up supplies since the island, like all public riding places, expects you to clean up after your horse in the parking area.

Chesapeake and Ohio Canal

This 185-mile long canal is a unique riding experience. The canal, originally intended to connect the Chesapeake Bay with the Ohio River, never reached its objective. However, the area is now a beautiful national park along the Potomac River from Washington, D.C., through the Maryland countryside. Riders are welcome but need to be sure to stay in a gait no faster than a slow trot. Camping is available but the park does not have horse rentals.

Shenandoah National Park

Like many of the national parks, Shenandoah allows you to bring your own horse. In addition, there is a resident stable that rents horses and guides rides. The park has 150 miles of horseback riding trails along its fire roads. There are no overnight horse facilities at Shenandoah—this is a day ride location only. You might be able to convince park officials to give you a backcountry camping permit but it's discouraged since horses are expected to be kept on the horse-designated trails.

Mammoth Cave National Park

This park is located in south central Kentucky and offers 60 miles of horseback riding trails. There are horse-friendly campsite areas where water is readily available. The park is home to more than seventy endangered and threatened species. Of course, one of the most interesting features of

Mammoth Cave National Park is the cave itself, which obviously cannot be explored by horseback!

St. Croix National Scenic Riverway

This gorgeous part of the country lies on the Wisconsin/Minnesota border. Several opportunities for miles of riding trails exist in the St. Croix State Forest, Wild River State Park, and the Governor Knowles State Forest. These are bring-your-own-horse trails that wind through forests and along the lovely St. Croix River Valley.

ALERT!

Bring enough grain for your horse for the extent of the trip plus several days extra—if you are going outside your region, you might not be able to find the brand of grain you normally feed. A trip is stressful enough on even the calmest of horses; it's not a time to be switching grains.

Theodore Roosevelt National Park

This 71,000-acre park in the North Dakota Badlands was created in honor of the twenty-sixth president of the United States. It's open to horse use; either bring your own horse or rent one from a trail ride outfit that operates in the park. This country is home to bison, wild horses, rattlesnakes, and other wildlife that can be fascinating and dangerous. You will need to carry in your own water for yourself and potentially for your horse as well. Free permits are available for backcountry overnight camping.

Glacier National Park

This is the heart of Montana where stock horses are a way of life. The park is open to all manner of riding but you need to reserve ahead for larger groups. There are serious rules and regulations to follow, and you need to know about backcountry riding to be safe and enjoy a tremendous ride through this national park.

Grand Teton National Park

Grand Teton National Park near Jackson Hole, Wyoming, offers several riding options. You can bring your own horse or there are various horse rental facilities in different areas of the park such as Colter Bay Cabins or Flagg Ranch Resort or the Triangle X Ranch.

King's Canyon National Park

This park, and the nearby Sequoia National Forest in central California, are open to horseback riders. They are classic backcountry trails and offer fair warnings about a prevalence of black bears, which means you need to know how to store food in a bear-proof fashion. Trail conditions are available from the park's Web site; there is also a list of descriptions of the various trails and their level of horse-friendliness. Riding in winter is highly discouraged and requires considerable experience. The wildlife, giant sequoias, and countryside make this area particularly breathtaking.

Organ Pipe Cactus National Monument

This Arizona park is home to classic desert country. Park rangers at the visitor center can help you plan a safe trip that is sensitive to the wildlife and terrain of this environment. As with most national parks, an inexpensive (usually $5 or so) backcountry riding permit is required.

When trailering a horse, always carry a halter and lead rope in your pickup within easy reach. Even if your horse wears a halter in the trailer, stick an extra one behind the driver's seat—in an accident, the halter might have to be cut off, and you will be happy you have an intact one handy.

Dude Ranches

Remember the movie *City Slickers*? So-called "dude ranches" are a well-organized group of western ranches that offer exactly the kind of opportunity that Billy Crystal and his city friends experienced (although typically without the gun shooting and spontaneous calf-delivering, but who knows!). The bigger, more developed dude ranches often offer lots of horseback riding, much of it with a purpose—moving cattle from one grazing area to another and checking fence lines.

The beauty of dude ranch vacationing is that they usually offer lots of other activities as well so the whole family or group of friends can enjoy the same vacation spot but those not interested in horses can do other activities. These activities could include hiking, wildlife viewing and photography, trips into the nearest cities and towns, or just lounging around in the Jacuzzi on the deck reading a book and occasionally looking up at stunning mountainous views.

There are hundreds of these popular vacation destinations so research them well to pick the one that best suits your vacation dreams.

FACT

Dude ranches are pretty well organized in the hospitality department. They have a couple of associations that they can join and that you can research to find the dude ranch that is best for your vacation. Here are two: The Dude Ranchers' Association, 1122 12th Street, P.O. Box 2307, Cody, WY 82414, ☎(307) 587-2339, ✍*www.duderanch.org* and the associated site, ✍*www.duderanches.com*. These sites not only list hundreds of dude ranches around the country, but they also provide tips on choosing and enjoying a dude ranch vacation.

The Big City

You're in the city for a few days and need a horse fix. It's not impossible. New York City, London, and most of the big cities of the world have been home to horses far longer than automobiles have been around. Check the phone book or ask the concierge at your hotel to locate a place where you can indulge your horse interests for an hour or an afternoon.

The Claremont Riding Academy in midtown Manhattan rents horses to ride the 6 miles of bridle paths that have laced through Central Park since the park was built. You usually need to reserve a horse at least a few days in advance. Contact the academy at 175 W. 89th Street, New York, NY 10024, ✆(212) 724-5100.

In London, ride along Hyde Park in the shadow of Buckingham Palace where you might even see the palace guards on horseback. Or in Wimbledon Common and Richmond Park on the outskirts of the city. Check the British Horse Society Web site (✍*www.bhs.org.uk*) to find a list of stables and what they offer, from hacks through Hyde Park to jumping lessons.

ALERT!

Although you should certainly bring your cell phone on trail rides, don't rely on it to be your only source of help in an emergency. Cell phones don't always work in the places you really need them to! Bring the supplies you might need for you and your horse to be as comfortable as possible in an emergency situation while you await help to come along or work your way out of the woods or off the trail to find help.

Ride All Over the World

There really is hardly a spot in the world where you couldn't make riding horses a significant part of your vacation. With a little legwork and some online research, you can come up with just the right skill level and amount of riding for you. Ask your horse friends as well, you'd be surprised how many will have fascinating tales of riding the beaches in Jamaica, going by burro into the Grand Canyon, or taking a trail ride through the rainforest.

Private Trail Riding Facilities

In most out-of-town areas, a breeze through the phone book under "horses" or "trail riding" will come up with one or two opportunities to go out on a guided trail ride for an hour or two. One way to find trail riding places and to get recommendations for the ones with the best horses, best trails, and safest approaches is to contact a local tack shop. Tack shops know every horse facility within a 50-mile range of the location.

Riding in Europe

European riding vacations are becoming popular and well organized. You can ride along the coast of Ireland, take jumping lessons interspersed with hacks through the woods in England, ride Andalusians in Spain or Portugal, take dressage lessons from the masters in Germany, the possibilities are endless. Search online under "riding horses in Europe" and you will be led to dozens of sites with organized tours all over Europe.

Iceland

Nothing is more fascinating than watching an Icelandic horse in action. These pony-sized powerhouses can carry an adult rider with ease. You can ride in the annual sheep roundup or help herd the horses back in from pasture after the summer. Check out the Web site *www.icelandadventure.com* to learn lots about the possibilities of riding in Iceland.

Even if you don't *plan* to ride on your vacation, pack a pair of riding jeans or breeches. You just never know when you'll get the urge!

Traveling for Clinics

Another way to enjoy horses on vacation is to combine education with fun. If you are planning a vacation, check out clinic offerings in the area you're going to. You can either check the Web sites of your favorite clinicians or locate a local horse magazine and see what's listed in their calendar. This is a great way to explore local horse culture in the area you are visiting. Bring a chair, a nice lunch, and for $25 or so you can spend a day watching horses and riders learn together. And you can meet lifelong friends who have the same interest in improving their horsemanship as you do. If you can bring your horse along, so much the better!

Chapter 20

Moving Up

You have become comfortable in the walk, trot, and canter. You know how to ask for these basic gaits and other movement—backing, lateral work—from your horse. You are comfortable riding with a few other riders, either on the trail or in the ring. Now it's probably time to challenge yourself further. You can do that in a number of ways.

Beyond the Basics

The most fundamental way to move up in horseback riding is to just keep sharpening your riding skill and move beyond the basics. Every discipline has higher levels to achieve. Once you can walk, trot, and canter your horse exactly when you want to and at exactly the speed you want, you are ready to take those basic gaits and refine and expand them to things like flying lead changes and extended and collected trot.

FACT

Horse shows and competitions are rated. A "local" show is the lowest level, drawing from a smaller net of horse-and-rider teams, and probably has a small attendance. The chances of a beginner being successful at a locally rated show are logically higher compared to the upper level "A-rated" shows that draw on large numbers of international competitors who have trained with the best known trainers in the world.

Moving up might mean simply dropping out of what you have been doing with your horse and trying something new. If that doesn't sound appealing, you can try learning about something new while continuing your current show schedule, trail riding plans, or whatever it is you are currently involved in.

Do your homework when it comes to considering any discipline change with your horse. Start by reading everything you can get your hands on. Local and regional magazines and newspapers focus on different aspects of riding and horses each month, sometimes the same month every year. Find out the editorial schedule (these magazines often publish it on their Web site) and look for that upcoming issue or get last year's copy. The good thing about these focused issues is that they also are packed with advertisers who focus on that discipline. You can find out about the discipline as well as learning about barns, instructors, and horses for sale that are involved in that discipline as well.

Up Your Circuit

Another way to move up in the horse world is to increase the level of your competition. If you have been showing in the local circuit, move up to the statewide circuit. From there, you can go to the regional circuit, then to the national, and on to international—the sky's the limit! Of course, with each level you move up to, the competition is more intense. If you are winning locally, your competition is with the local cream of the crop. The number of competitors gets much larger when you broaden your market beyond local riders. The cost of competing becomes higher as well, from higher entry fees to higher costs of travel. But if you think you are ready and have the time, funds, and inclination, widening your competitive market is a simple way to move up in the show world.

If you have been cleaning house in the Western pleasure classes in the horse shows, relish your success for a while. But at some point, you will get bored toting home all those blue ribbons. Winning all the time means it's time for a challenge. If you can't wait for the riders around you to step up to the plate, you need to make a change yourself. Start educating a young horse using the skills you are exhibiting by winning blue ribbons with your seasoned mount. Or change your show focus; for example, you can give the pleasure classes a break and show in equitation classes where you are the focus of the judging not your horse. Everything you do differently will increase your riding skills.

It can't be said enough—unless this is a profession for you and you are doing horse-related things to earn a living, FUN is the operative word. Oh, every minute is certainly not going to be a blast. But being involved with horses—even amidst the frustration and exhaustion—is just plain fun. If you don't find riding fun but you really know you want to be involved with horses, it's time to explore a different way of being involved.

If you are considering a new discipline or a new circuit, attend some events without a horse. Go, relax, and just watch. You will be able to get a clear sense of whether you could envision yourself in the atmosphere of this type of riding. Trail rides are a little hard to watch but there's almost always opportunities to volunteer. People are needed at checkpoints to help care for horses and riders; you might be able to be a driver and drive the judge around to various judged obstacles.

New Horse

One way to progress in your riding is to ride a different horse. In fact, riding as many different horses as you can is a great way to improve your riding.

Don't worry, that doesn't mean you have buy a new horse and/or sell the horse you own! There are plenty of ways to ride other horses without giving up the one you have. It isn't necessary to abandon your current mount. In fact, what you learn as you move up and progress in your riding you can bring back to your favorite horse and work on together.

Changing horses might be as simple as asking your instructor if you can ride a horse at a higher level in your lessons. Most active lesson barns keep horses in different levels of education, background, schooling in certain disciplines, or horses simply of various ages for different levels of students. Your instructor will probably suggest you change horses before you even think of it. It's to his or her advantage to keep you interested in taking lessons.

FACT

Age is a real consideration. One nice thing about horseback riding is that you tend to stay more flexible and more physically fit even with age just by the sheer nature of what is involved in being around horses. But it cannot be denied that what we do without fear or consideration of danger when we are twenty is probably quite a bit different from what we are willing to do when we are forty-five. Don't let age be your overriding concern, but don't feel like you need to act like a twenty-year-old your entire horse life either!

If you trail ride with a buddy a lot, suggest switching horses once in a while. This can be a fun way to spice up your ride. When you really progress in your horsemanship, you won't be interested in letting someone else ride your horse, but if your good buddy rides with the same approach you do then you might consider it. Of course, you need to feel comfortable about the idea of riding your friend's horse!

An interesting exercise is to switch horses partway through the ride. Horses are often hard to move on the way out on the trail and hard to hold back on the way home. Switch with your friend halfway out and then switch back to your own horses halfway back to the barn or the trailer. See whether your horses act differently under different riders. If so—either better or worse—try to figure out what you are doing differently. It can be an eye opening experience!

When you ride the same horse all the time, you can become dull to the details. A different horse offers a new perspective. Your legs will probably sit differently on him. He will respond differently to the bit, bend differently. It's like driving a new car—in your own car you know where the windshield wiper switch is, the style of shift lever, and can operate those things without even thinking consciously about them. In a new car, you need to look for the right dials and figure out how they work (preferably before you are moving!). Of course, riding a horse involves the additional complication of another being with thoughts and feelings about everything you're doing with him.

ALERT!

The first time you get on a different horse, keep it simple. Don't ask for a lot from the horse; go with the flow. Go into hyperawareness mode and take the opportunity to really feel what's going on underneath you.

New Instructor

If you decide to change disciplines altogether, you probably will have to change instructors anyway. But even if you decide to stay within your discipline, perhaps one way to move up to a higher level is to change instructors.

Most instructors can actually teach well beyond their own level of ability but realistically an instructor can only take a student so far. And sometimes by simply changing your instructor, you will get enough of a fresh perspective and new exercises and approaches that it can keep your enthusiasm going without ever having to change disciplines or horses.

If you do move to a new instructor, try to leave your former instructor on a good note. The horse world tends to be quite small, and you never know when you will run across your former instructor—or his or her partner, daughter, or aunt!

Be upfront about why you are changing, especially so he or she will know that it's more about you than about the instructor. If you can do this diplomatically, you could get a good recommendation of some new instructors to try out. And if things don't work out with the new person, you can go back to your former instructor.

ALERT!

Don't change what you are doing just because someone else is telling you to. If you feel deep in your heart that it's time for a change, go for it. But if your heart isn't in it, what's the point? And if you are the type of rider who likes things calm and on an even keel, don't switch from your Western pleasure show circuit to a fast-paced activity like barrel racing! If you get hurt, you can easily lose your confidence and perhaps your desire to ride at all.

Progressing Within Your Discipline

When you first started out riding, you probably were so excited you never imagined that you could possibly get bored with anything that had to do with horses. But few people can do the same thing for years and years and years without needing to work a little at keeping it exciting and interesting.

If you are bored, you can be certain your horse is bored! Remember, he's the tagalong half of this partnership—it isn't his idea to do whatever it is you have chosen to do. In fact, it's pretty clear that all things considered, a horse would be quite content to hang out in a few acres of pasture with a few buddies for the rest of his life without ever jumping a jump, running a barrel pattern, or even getting groomed! They might enjoy it when they do it, but they probably wouldn't choose to work that hard without a mountain lion on their tail—it's just not their nature.

Think about shaking up your horse life a little before you ever get to the bored stage. When you really begin to be comfortable with something, add a twist to it or stick with it while beginning to learn something different.

If you decide to change horses as your way of "moving up," move down in your level for an event or two. Get used to your new horse. Even if he is experienced and jumping 4' fences at home, do the 3'6" height division at the show. You want to set yourself up for success—not start out with your new horse challenged to the max.

Show Progress

Most show disciplines—reining, pleasure classes, jumping—have built-in levels of competition to help keep riders progressing. You can start out in the novice division, move through the amateur division and New Discipline, and if you really become horse absorbed, the professional divisions. ("Professional" in almost any sport means you are making money in the sport—in the horse world, it's usually as a trainer or instructor.)

Grand Prix Aspirations

Dressage competitions innately offer many levels that you and your horse can rise through. Most dressage riders go through several horses as they progress—horses that are good at the lower levels of dressage might never have the athleticism needed for the higher levels. The top levels of dressage are achieved by comparatively few so you can always have that carrot out in front of you.

FACT

There are nine levels of dressage training and competition that you and your horse can train in: Training, First, Second, Third, Fourth, Prix St. Georges, Intermediate 1, Intermediate 2, and Grand Prix. Don't be in any hurry to get through each level—it can take years to move out of the early stages and most horses or riders never achieve the upper levels, especially Grand Prix.

New Heights

If your horsemanship pursuits have led you to jumping, "moving up" can simply mean making the jumps more difficult. They can get higher or wider or involve complications such as water in front or behind. Jumps can be placed in more complicated series or have potentially distracting things on either side of the jump. Besides the course itself, you can alter your jumping discipline and move into cross country, eventing, or even fox hunting to challenge you and your horse.

ESSENTIAL

Changing to a completely new discipline can be a lot of fun, but you want to think carefully about whether that much change is necessary to rev up your and your horse's enthusiasm. A completely new discipline can feel like starting from scratch, which can be discouraging. Changing within your current discipline might be the better idea. Or maybe not— the point is to consider everything.

New Discipline

Maybe after careful consideration of all the possibilities, you have decided you are ready to completely change the discipline you and your horse are involved in. The important thing is thinking it over and weighing the pros and cons of staying with the discipline you have been working in. Here are a couple of questions to ask yourself.

Why Do You Want to Change?

Has the routine of my chosen riding discipline become boring? Am I tired of living out of a horse trailer and being at horse show barns most weekends of the show season? Have I begun to be less interested in the kinds of people attracted to this discipline? Does my horse seem to be sour to it all too?

These are the kinds of questions to ask to figure out just what it is about your current discipline that is turning you away from it. Then you can decide whether it's time to find a completely new thing to do with your horse.

Perhaps a smaller change would do the trick. For instance, instead of staying in your horse trailer's living quarters, you should sell your trailer, buy a smaller one, and stay in hotels nearby the show grounds. If the people involved in horse showing are no longer sustaining your horse camaraderie needs, you will want to find a nonshowing type discipline to become involved in.

ALERT!

Don't forget, when you change disciplines, you will most likely also need to change your entire wardrobe, including your horse's tack. Borrow what you can for a while, buy used when you have to, and wait and see if you really like the new activity enough to buy all new clothes and equipment. You might even need to change your horse!

Have You Become Frightened?

Many people who fly in airplanes a lot go through a period of being afraid of flying. Frequent flyers are often surprised by this seemingly sudden change but it's quite natural and common. Some get over it easily on their own, while some need professional help to get over their fear.

Seasoned performers can go through stage fright as well. Horse competitors can fall into this performance jitters category. Even high-level competitors will admit to having butterflies in their stomachs before they enter the show ring—in fact, many find that the butterflies are what get them revved up for the performance. Some, however, get to the point of nausea and near hyperventilation, which makes it difficult to perform at all.

If you have found that entering the show ring has become almost nauseating to you, you have a couple of options. One option is to find some professional help. For those who take competition very seriously—especially those competing on a professional level—a sports psychologist is the person you would turn to. For others—those who are doing this for "fun"—turn to your instructor or hire a coach who is well-schooled in your chosen discipline. At the very least, team up with a buddy who competes and have her help you through the jitters.

If 4-foot jumps suddenly start looking like impossible 10-footers to you, go down a notch in the height. There's no rule that says just because you've jumped 4-footers, you can never jump a 3'6" jump again! You need to do what is right for you. The other option to consider is changing disciplines. But if the show ring is causing you lots of anxiety, you might simply want to look for a discipline that isn't focused on showing.

Keep one thing in mind—there's no one saying you need to move up at all! If you trail ride recreationally and do nothing more than walk your horse through woods and fields, and you and the horse you ride like it that way, who's saying you need to change a thing? Although most people who are involved with horses feel differently, horses are not one of life's necessities. Figure out what you like about being involved with horses—and enjoy it!

Appendix A

Catalogs

Order from just one of these catalogs, and you will probably start getting them all. Once you get into horses, you'll look forward to a catalog stuffed mailbox! Virtually all of them have Web sites that you can order from, but the catalogs are great fun to stack on the floor beside your favorite chair and browse through to your heart's content.

American Livestock Supply
General horse supplies
613 Atlas Ave.
Madison, WI 53714
✆(800) 356-0700
🖉www.americanlivestock.com

Back in the Saddle
Gifts, apparel, and supplies
570 Turner Drive Ste D
Durango, CO 81303
✆(800) 865-2478
🖉www.backinthesaddle.com

The Barn Depot
Stable supplies
489 Neck Road
Lancaster, MA 01523
✆(978) 368-9100
🖉www.barndepot.com

Chamisa Ridge
Herbals and gifts
3212A Richards Lane
Santa Fe, NM 87507
✆(800) 743-3188
🖉www.chamisaridge.com

Country Supply
General supplies
5833 118th Ave
Ottumwa, IA 52501
✆(800) 637-6721

Dover Saddlery
Horse and rider apparel
and supplies
P.O. Box 1100
Littleton, MA 01460
✆(800) 989-1500
🖉www.doversaddlery.com

Drysdales
Western wear and gear
1555 N. 107th East Ave.
Tulsa, OK 74116
✆(800) 444-6481
🖉www.drysdales.com

Farnam
Farm equipment
P.O. Box 34820
Phoenix, AZ 85067
✆(800) 267-5211
🖉www.farnamequipment.com

Exclusively Equine
Gifts and books
P.O. Box 4038
Lexington, KY 40544
✆(800) 582-5604
🖉www.ExclusivelyEquine.com

Ishetar
Riding vacations
Sorlaskeid 26
220 Hafnarfjordur
Lynghalsi 3
110 Reykjavik, Iceland
✆(+354) 555-7025

Jeffers
Livestock equipment
and supplies
P.O. Box 100
Dothan, AL 36301
(800) 533-3377
www.jeffersequine.com

Knight Equestrian Books
P.O. Box 78
Edgecomb, ME 04556
(207) 882-5494
www.knightbooks.com

KV Vet Supply
General supplies
3190 N Road
David City, NE 68632
(800) 423-8211
www.kvvet.com

Nasco Farm and Ranch
901 Janesville Ave.
Fort Atkinson, WI 53538
(800) 558-9595
www.eNASCO.com

National Roper's Supply
410 S FM 51
Decatur, TX 76234
(940) 627-0101
www.nationalropers
supply.com

O'Halloran Co.
High fashion apparel
65 Main St
Millerton, NY 12546
(866) 789-4785
www.ohalloranco.com

Robin Bledsoe, Bookseller
1640 Massachusetts Ave.
Cambridge, MA 02138
(617) 576-3634
www.abebooks.com

Rod's
Western apparel and gifts
3099 Silver Drive
Columbus, OH 43224
(800) 325-8508
www.rods.com

Running Bear
Trail riding equipment
1348 Township Road 256
Kitts Hill, OH 45645
(800) 533-BEAR
www.runningbear.com

Schneider Saddlery
General horse and rider supplies
8255 East Washington Street
Chagrin Falls, OH 44023
(800) 365-1311

Sergeant's

Gear and apparel
13600 Stemmons Fwy
Farmers Branch, TX 75234
☎(800) 383-3669
✍*www.sergeantswestern.com*

Show Stable Artisans

Equestrian jewelry
5 "W" Street
Nantasket Beach
Hull, MA 02045
☎(800) 701-2710
✍*www.equestrianjewelry.com*

Smith Brothers

Western gear and apparel
P.O. Box 2700
Denton, TX 76202
☎(800) 433-5558
✍*www.smithbrothers.com*

Soda Creek Western Outfitters

Western wear
P.O. Box 4343
335 Lincoln Avenue
Steamboat Springs, CO 80477
☎(800) 824-8426

State Line Tack

General horse and rider supplies
☎(888) 839-9640
✍*www.statelinetack.com*

Valley Vet Supply

General horse supplies
1118 Pony Express Highway
P.O. Box 504
Marysville, KS 66508
☎(800) 356-1005
✍*www.valleyvet.com*

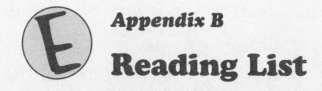

Appendix B

Reading List

The following books are great reading material for those times when you are only able to be an armchair rider.

Balzotti, Jim. *Jim Balzotti's Best Guest Ranches and Horseback Riding Vacations.* (Pembroke, MA: Balzotti Publications, 1999).

Benedik, Linda, and Veronica Wirth. *Yoga for Equestrians.* (North Pomfret, VT: Trafalgar Square Publishing, 2000).

Brannaman, Buck. *Groundwork.* (Marina Del Ray, CA: Rancho Deluxe Design, 1997).

Dorrance, Bill, with Leslie Desmond. *True Horsemanship Through Feel.* (Novato, CA: Diamond Lu Productions, 1999).

Dorrance, Tom. *True Unity.* (Tuscarora, NM: Give-It-a-Go Enterprises, 1987).

Hassler, Jill Keiser. *Beyond the Mirrors.* (Quarryville, PA: Goals Unlimited, 1988).

Hill, Cherry. *101 Arena Exercises.* (North Adams, MA: Storey Books, 1995).

Hogg, Abigail. *The Horse Behaviour Handbook.* (Devon, England: David & Charles, 2003).

Hunt, Ray. *Think Harmony with Horses.* (Tuscarora, NM: Give-It-a-Go Enterprises, 1978).

Kimball, Cheryl. *Mindful Horsemanship.* (Middleton, NH: Carriage House Publishing, 2002).

Lilley, Claire. *Schooling with Ground Poles.* (North Pomfret, VT: Trafalgar Square Publishing, 2003).

Livingston, Phil. *Team Penning.* (Colorado Springs, CO: Western Horseman, 2002).

Marks, Kelly. *Ride with Confidence.* (Devon, England: David & Charles, 2004).

Murdoch, Wendy. *Simplify Your Riding.* (Middleton, NH: Carriage House Publishing, 2004).

Ocko, Stephanie. *Adventure Vacations: A 50-State Guide to Rock Climbing, Horseback Riding, Spelunking, Whitewater Rafting, Snorkeling, Hang Gliding and Ballooning.* (New York, NY: Carol Publishing, 1995).

O'Connor, Sally. *Common Sense Dressage.* (Middletown, MD: Half Halt Press, 1990).

Pate, Curt, with Fran D. Smith. *Ranch Horsemanship.* (Colorado Springs, CO: Western Horseman, 2004).

Pelicano, Rick, with Lauren Tjaden. *Bombproof Your Horse.* (North Pomfret, VT: Trafalgar Square Publishing, 2004).

Podhasky, Alois. *My Horse, My Teachers.* (North Pomfret, VT: Trafalgar Square Press, 1997).

Savoie, Jane. *Cross-Train Your Horse.* (North Pomfret, VT: Trafalgar Square Publishing, 1998).

Skipper, Lesley. *Realize Your Horse's True Potential.* (North Pomfret, VT: Trafalgar Square Publishing, 2003).

Swift, Sally. *Centered Riding.* (North Pomfret, VT: Trafalgar Square Publishing, 1985).

Trott, David, and Penny Hillsdon. *Preparing for a Dressage Test.* (London, England: J. A. Allen, 2001).

Trott, David, and Penny Hillsdon. *Riding a Dressage Test.* (London, England: J. A. Allen, 2001).

Wright, Ed, and Martha Wright. *Barrel Racing the Wright Way.* (Colorado Springs, CO: Western Horseman, 1999).

Index

THE EVERYTHING SERIES!

BUSINESS & PERSONAL FINANCE

Everything® Budgeting Book
Everything® Business Planning Book
Everything® Coaching and Mentoring Book
Everything® Fundraising Book
Everything® Get Out of Debt Book
Everything® Grant Writing Book
Everything® Home-Based Business Book
Everything® Homebuying Book, 2nd Ed.
Everything® Homeselling Book, 2nd Ed.
Everything® Investing Book, 2nd Ed.
Everything® Landlording Book
Everything® Leadership Book
Everything® Managing People Book
Everything® Negotiating Book
Everything® Online Business Book
Everything® Personal Finance Book
Everything® Personal Finance in Your 20s
    and 30s Book
Everything® Project Management Book
Everything® Real Estate Investing Book
Everything® Robert's Rules Book, $7.95
Everything® Selling Book
Everything® Start Your Own Business Book
Everything® Wills & Estate Planning Book

COOKING

Everything® Barbecue Cookbook
Everything® Bartender's Book, $9.95
Everything® Chinese Cookbook
Everything® Cocktail Parties and Drinks
    Book
Everything® College Cookbook
Everything® Cookbook
Everything® Cooking for Two Cookbook
Everything® Diabetes Cookbook
Everything® Easy Gourmet Cookbook
Everything® Fondue Cookbook
Everything® Gluten-Free Cookbook

Everything® Grilling Cookbook
Everything® Healthy Meals in Minutes
    Cookbook
Everything® Holiday Cookbook
Everything® Indian Cookbook
Everything® Italian Cookbook
Everything® Low-Carb Cookbook
Everything® Low-Fat High-Flavor Cookbook
Everything® Low-Salt Cookbook
Everything® Meals for a Month Cookbook
Everything® Mediterranean Cookbook
Everything® Mexican Cookbook
Everything® One-Pot Cookbook
Everything® Pasta Cookbook
Everything® Quick Meals Cookbook
Everything® Slow Cooker Cookbook
Everything® Slow Cooking for a Crowd
    Cookbook
Everything® Soup Cookbook
Everything® Thai Cookbook
Everything® Vegetarian Cookbook
Everything® Wine Book, 2nd Ed.

CRAFT SERIES

Everything® Crafts—Baby Scrapbooking
Everything® Crafts—Bead Your Own Jewelry
Everything® Crafts—Create Your Own
    Greeting Cards
Everything® Crafts—Easy Projects
Everything® Crafts—Polymer Clay for
    Beginners
Everything® Crafts—Rubber Stamping
    Made Easy
Everything® Crafts—Wedding Decorations
    and Keepsakes

HEALTH

Everything® Alzheimer's Book
Everything® Diabetes Book
Everything® Health Guide to Controlling
    Anxiety

Everything® Hypnosis Book
Everything® Low Cholesterol Book
Everything® Massage Book
Everything® Menopause Book
Everything® Nutrition Book
Everything® Reflexology Book
Everything® Stress Management Book

HISTORY

Everything® American Government Book
Everything® American History Book
Everything® Civil War Book
Everything® Irish History & Heritage Book
Everything® Middle East Book

HOBBIES & GAMES

Everything® Blackjack Strategy Book
Everything® Brain Strain Book, $9.95
Everything® Bridge Book
Everything® Candlemaking Book
Everything® Card Games Book
Everything® Card Tricks Book, $9.95
Everything® Cartooning Book
Everything® Casino Gambling Book, 2nd Ed.
Everything® Chess Basics Book
Everything® Craps Strategy Book
Everything® Crossword and Puzzle Book
Everything® Crossword Challenge Book
Everything® Cryptograms Book, $9.95
Everything® Digital Photography Book
Everything® Drawing Book
Everything® Easy Crosswords Book
Everything® Family Tree Book, 2nd Ed.
Everything® Games Book, 2nd Ed.
Everything® Knitting Book
Everything® Knots Book
Everything® Photography Book
Everything® Poker Strategy Book
Everything® Pool & Billiards Book
Everything® Quilting Book
Everything® Scrapbooking Book

All Everything® books are priced at $12.95 or $14.95, unless otherwise stated. Prices subject to change without notice.

Everything® Sewing Book
Everything® Test Your IQ Book, $9.95
Everything® Travel Crosswords Book, $9.95
Everything® Woodworking Book
Everything® Word Games Challenge Book
Everything® Word Search Book

HOME IMPROVEMENT

Everything® Feng Shui Book
Everything® Feng Shui Decluttering Book,
    $9.95
Everything® Fix-It Book
Everything® Homebuilding Book
Everything® Lawn Care Book
Everything® Organize Your Home Book

EVERYTHING® *KIDS'* BOOKS

All titles are $6.95

Everything® Kids' Animal Puzzle & Activity
    Book
Everything® Kids' Baseball Book, 3rd Ed.
Everything® Kids' Bible Trivia Book
Everything® Kids' Bugs Book
Everything® Kids' Christmas Puzzle
    & Activity Book
Everything® Kids' Cookbook
Everything® Kids' Crazy Puzzles Book
Everything® Kids' Dinosaurs Book
Everything® Kids' Gross Jokes Book
Everything® Kids' Gross Puzzle and
    Activity Book
Everything® Kids' Halloween Puzzle
    & Activity Book
Everything® Kids' Hidden Pictures Book
Everything® Kids' Joke Book
Everything® Kids' Knock Knock Book
Everything® Kids' Math Puzzles Book
Everything® Kids' Mazes Book
Everything® Kids' Money Book
Everything® Kids' Nature Book
Everything® Kids' Puzzle Book
Everything® Kids' Riddles & Brain Teasers Book
Everything® Kids' Science Experiments Book
Everything® Kids' Sharks Book
Everything® Kids' Soccer Book
Everything® Kids' Travel Activity Book

KIDS' STORY BOOKS

Everything® Fairy Tales Book

LANGUAGE

Everything® Conversational Japanese Book
    (with CD), $19.95
Everything® French Phrase Book, $9.95
Everything® French Verb Book, $9.95
Everything® Inglés Book
Everything® Learning French Book
Everything® Learning German Book
Everything® Learning Italian Book
Everything® Learning Latin Book
Everything® Learning Spanish Book
Everything® Sign Language Book
Everything® Spanish Grammar Book
Everything® Spanish Practice Book
    (with CD), $19.95
Everything® Spanish Phrase Book, $9.95
Everything® Spanish Verb Book, $9.95

MUSIC

Everything® Drums Book (with CD), $19.95
Everything® Guitar Book
Everything® Home Recording Book
Everything® Playing Piano and Keyboards
    Book
Everything® Reading Music Book (with CD),
    $19.95
Everything® Rock & Blues Guitar Book
    (with CD), $19.95
Everything® Songwriting Book

NEW AGE

Everything® Astrology Book, 2nd Ed.
Everything® Dreams Book, 2nd Ed.
Everything® Ghost Book
Everything® Love Signs Book, $9.95
Everything® Numerology Book
Everything® Paganism Book
Everything® Palmistry Book
Everything® Psychic Book
Everything® Reiki Book
Everything® Tarot Book
Everything® Wicca and Witchcraft Book

PARENTING

Everything® Baby Names Book
Everything® Baby Shower Book
Everything® Baby's First Food Book
Everything® Baby's First Year Book
Everything® Birthing Book
Everything® Breastfeeding Book
Everything® Father-to-Be Book
Everything® Father's First Year Book
Everything® Get Ready for Baby Book
Everything® Get Your Baby to Sleep Book,
    $9.95
Everything® Getting Pregnant Book
Everything® Homeschooling Book
Everything® Mother's First Year Book
Everything® Parent's Guide to Children
    and Divorce
Everything® Parent's Guide to Children
    with ADD/ADHD
Everything® Parent's Guide to Children
    with Asperger's Syndrome
Everything® Parent's Guide to Children
    with Autism
Everything® Parent's Guide to Children with
    Bipolar Disorder
Everything® Parent's Guide to Children
    with Dyslexia
Everything® Parent's Guide to Positive
    Discipline
Everything® Parent's Guide to Raising a
    Successful Child
Everything® Parent's Guide to Tantrums
Everything® Parent's Guide to the Overweight
    Child
Everything® Parent's Guide to the Strong-
    Willed Child
Everything® Parenting a Teenager Book
Everything® Potty Training Book, $9.95
Everything® Pregnancy Book, 2nd Ed.
Everything® Pregnancy Fitness Book
Everything® Pregnancy Nutrition Book
Everything® Pregnancy Organizer, $15.00
Everything® Toddler Book
Everything® Tween Book
Everything® Twins, Triplets, and More Book

All Everything® books are priced at $12.95 or $14.95, unless otherwise stated. Prices subject to change without notice.

PETS

Everything® Cat Book
Everything® Dachshund Book
Everything® Dog Book
Everything® Dog Health Book
Everything® Dog Training and Tricks Book
Everything® German Shepherd Book
Everything® Golden Retriever Book
Everything® Horse Book
Everything® Horseback Riding Book
Everything® Labrador Retriever Book
Everything® Poodle Book
Everything® Pug Book
Everything® Puppy Book
Everything® Rottweiler Book
Everything® Small Dogs Book
Everything® Tropical Fish Book
Everything® Yorkshire Terrier Book

REFERENCE

Everything® Car Care Book
Everything® Classical Mythology Book
Everything® Computer Book
Everything® Divorce Book
Everything® Einstein Book
Everything® Etiquette Book, 2nd Ed.
Everything® Inventions and Patents Book
Everything® Mafia Book
Everything® Philosophy Book
Everything® Psychology Book
Everything® Shakespeare Book

RELIGION

Everything® Angels Book
Everything® Bible Book
Everything® Buddhism Book
Everything® Catholicism Book
Everything® Christianity Book
Everything® Jewish History & Heritage Book
Everything® Judaism Book
Everything® Koran Book
Everything® Prayer Book
Everything® Saints Book

Everything® Torah Book
Everything® Understanding Islam Book
Everything® World's Religions Book
Everything® Zen Book

SCHOOL & CAREERS

Everything® Alternative Careers Book
Everything® College Survival Book, 2nd Ed.
Everything® Cover Letter Book, 2nd Ed.
Everything® Get-a-Job Book
Everything® Guide to Starting and Running
    a Restaurant
Everything® Job Interview Book
Everything® New Teacher Book
Everything® Online Job Search Book
Everything® Paying for College Book
Everything® Practice Interview Book
Everything® Resume Book, 2nd Ed.
Everything® Study Book

SELF-HELP

Everything® Dating Book, 2nd Ed.
Everything® Great Sex Book
Everything® Kama Sutra Book
Everything® Self-Esteem Book

SPORTS & FITNESS

Everything® Fishing Book
Everything® Golf Instruction Book
Everything® Pilates Book
Everything® Running Book
Everything® Total Fitness Book
Everything® Weight Training Book
Everything® Yoga Book

TRAVEL

Everything® Family Guide to Hawaii
Everything® Family Guide to Las Vegas,
    2nd Ed.
Everything® Family Guide to New York City,
    2nd Ed.
Everything® Family Guide to RV Travel &
    Campgrounds

Everything® Family Guide to the Walt Disney
    World Resort®, Universal Studios®,
    and Greater Orlando, 4th Ed.
Everything® Family Guide to Cruise Vacations
Everything® Family Guide to the Caribbean
Everything® Family Guide to Washington
    D.C., 2nd Ed.
Everything® Guide to New England
Everything® Travel Guide to the Disneyland
    Resort®, California Adventure®,
    Universal Studios®, and the
    Anaheim Area

WEDDINGS

Everything® Bachelorette Party Book, $9.95
Everything® Bridesmaid Book, $9.95
Everything® Elopement Book, $9.95
Everything® Father of the Bride Book, $9.95
Everything® Groom Book, $9.95
Everything® Mother of the Bride Book, $9.95
Everything® Outdoor Wedding Book
Everything® Wedding Book, 3rd Ed.
Everything® Wedding Checklist, $9.95
Everything® Wedding Etiquette Book, $9.95
Everything® Wedding Organizer, $15.00
Everything® Wedding Shower Book, $9.95
Everything® Wedding Vows Book, $9.95
Everything® Weddings on a Budget Book,
    $9.95

WRITING

Everything® Creative Writing Book
Everything® Get Published Book
Everything® Grammar and Style Book
Everything® Guide to Writing a Book Proposal
Everything® Guide to Writing a Novel
Everything® Guide to Writing Children's Books
Everything® Guide to Writing Research Papers
Everything® Screenwriting Book
Everything® Writing Poetry Book
Everything® Writing Well Book

Available wherever books are sold!
To order, call 800-258-0929, or visit us at *www.everything.com*
Everything® and everything.com® are registered trademarks of F+W Publications, Inc.